SOCIAL MEDIA MARKETING 2020

FRANK DARRELL

COPYRIGHT

The trademarks that are used are without any consent, and the publication of the trademark is without permission or backing by the trademark owner. All trademarks and brands within this book are for clarifying purposes only and are the owned by the owners themselves, not affiliated with this document.

CONTENTS

INTRODUCTION

The difficulties confronting worldwide businesses and the individuals who lead them are presently, like never before, entwined in the immediate strengthening and contribution of clients and partners. The World Wide Web—portrayed by Sir Tim Berners-Lee as "an intelligent ocean of shared learning... made of the things we and our companions have seen, heard, accept or have made sense of"— has drastically quickened the shift to customer driven markets. For centuries, control has rested with those assets: first with land, then capital, and most as of late, data. In a socially associated commercial center, shared learning is currently developing as a definitive asset. Data needs to be free, and in these new markets it is: free of requirements on place, free of control on con-tent, and free of prohibitive access on utilization.

Social advancements, on a mass scale, interface individuals in manners that encourage sharing data, along these lines diminishing the open doors for commercial center misuse—regardless of whether by charging more than a contending provider for generally indistinguishable merchandise and ventures or charging anything at all for items that essentially don't work. Daylight is a ground-breaking disinfectant, and the aggregate learning that powers the Social Web is the daylight that sparkles in these new associated commercial centers. The Social Web drastically makes everything fair by making data plentiful, similarly as it additionally levels businesses and associations that work on the standards of making data rare.

The Social Web uncovered the great, the terrible, and the revolting, all the while raising up what works and putting down what doesn't without respect for the interests of a specific gathering. Web 2.0 innovations—communicated through social CRM, merchant relationship the executives, aggregate glorification, client driven help discussions, and networks where members participate in all types of social talk—act together to even out the market places of providers, makers, business and hierarchical pioneers, clients and partners. To again cite Sir Tim Berners-Lee, "If mistaken assumptions are the reason for huge numbers of the world's troubles, then (we can) work them out in the internet. Furthermore, having worked them out, we leave for the individuals who pursue a trail of our thinking and presumptions for them to receive, or right."

So in the case of supporting Unilever, P&G, and Nestlé, all working with Greenpeace to guarantee provider consistence in the utilization of maintainable palm oil and in this way lessening ecological harm in no-more extended "far away" places like Malaysia, or simply filling somebody's heart with joy run somewhat more easily by counteracting an espresso recolor through a basic advancement like Starbucks' "no sprinkle" mixing stick, the businesses and associations grasping social advances are conveying better arrangements—created through direct joint effort with clients and partners—to the world's hardships anyway enormous or small they might be. Contemporary businesses, cause-based associations, and administering specialists are progressively meeting the test of "opening up" and working with their clients and partners—often through a comparatively enabled and associated workforce—to convey plainly obvious worth that gets discussed. For these elements, their clients, providers, and partners are the new wellspring of future advancements and "marketing," and subsequently likewise the drivers of long haul development and achievement. This is the thing that social business is about.

CHAPTER 1
WHAT IS SOCIAL MEDIA MARKETING AND WHY IT IMPORTANT?

Defining Social Media Marketing

Social media marketing (SMM) is the utilization of social media sites and social systems to showcase an organization's items and administrations. Social media marketing gives organizations an approach to arrive at new clients, connect with existing clients, and advance their ideal culture, strategic, tone. Otherwise called "computerized marketing" and "e-marketing," social media marketing has direction fabricated information investigation instruments that enable advertisers to follow how effective their endeavors are.

Separating Social Media Marketing (SMM)

Social media sites enable advertisers to utilize a wide scope of strategies and procedures to advance content and have individuals draw in with it. Numerous social systems enable clients to give point by point land, statistic, and individual data, which will empower advertisers to tailor their messages to what is well on the way to reverberate with clients. Because Internet crowds can be preferable sectioned over increasingly conventional marketing channels, organizations can guarantee that they are concentrating their assets on the group of spectators that they need to target.

Social media marketing efforts have the upside of speaking to an expansive group of spectators without a moment's delay. For instance, a crusade could speak to present and forthcoming clients, representatives, bloggers, the media, the overall population, and different partners, (for example, outsider commentators or exchange gatherings). A portion of the measurements used to gauge the accomplishment of a social media marketing effort incorporate site reports, (for example, Google investigation), degree of profitability (by associating marketing to deals action), client reaction rates (how much clients post about an organization), and reach/virality (how much clients offer content).

Social Media Marketing Strategy

A significant technique utilized in social media marketing is to create messages and substance that individual clients will impart to their family, companions, and collaborators. This methodology depends on informal exchange and gives a few advantages. To begin with, it expands the message's span to systems and clients that a social media chief might not have had the option to get to something else. Second, shared substance conveys an understood underwriting when sent by somebody who the beneficiary knows and trusts.

Social media methodology includes the making of substance that is "clingy," implying that it will stand out enough to be noticed and increment the likelihood that the individual in question will direct an ideal activity, for example, buy an item or offer the substance with others. Advertisers make viral substance intended to spread between clients rapidly. Social media marketing ought to likewise urge clients to make and share their very own substance, for example, item audits or remarks (known as "earned media").

While social media marketing can give benefits, it additionally can make impediments that organizations might not have needed to manage something else. For instance, a viral video guaranteeing that an organization's item makes buyers become sick must be tended to by the organization, paying little mind to whether the case is valid or false. Regardless of whether an organization can sort the message out, buyers might be less inclined to buy from the organization later on.

Importance Of Social Media Marketing

Social media is rapidly turning out to be one of the most significant parts of computerized marketing, which gives mind blowing benefits that help arrive at a large number of clients around the world. What's more, if you are not having any significant bearing this gainful source, you are passing up a major opportunity a staggering marketing opportunity, as it makes it simple to get the message out about your item and mission.

Improved brand mindfulness

Social media is one of the most calm and gainful advanced marketing stages that can be utilized to build your business perceivability. To begin, make social media profiles for your business and start organizing with others. By applying a social media procedure, it will help you significantly increment your brand acknowledgment. By spending just a couple of hours out of every week, over 91% advertisers guaranteed that their social marketing endeavors significantly expanded their brand perceivability and elevated client experience. Without a doubt, having a social media page for your brand will profit your business and with a standard use, it can likewise deliver a wide group of spectators for your business in the blink of an eye.

Cost-effective

For a promoting technique, social media marketing is conceivably the most cost-effective way. Making a record and joining is free for practically all social systems administration stages. In any case, if you choose to utilize paid promoting on social media, consistently start small to perceive what you ought to anticipate. Being cost-effective is significant as it causes you accomplish a more noteworthy rate of profitability and hold a greater spending plan for other marketing and business installments. Just by contributing a minimal expenditure and time, you can significantly build your change rates and at last get an arrival on speculation on the cash that you fundamentally contributed.

Connect with your clients

Social media is a decent path for drawing in and connecting clients. The more you speak with the group of spectators, the more possibilities you have of transformation. Set up a two-route correspondence with your intended interest group so their desires are known and their advantage is provided food easily. In addition, correspondence and commitment with clients is one the approaches to win their consideration and pass on them your brand message. Along these lines, your brand will contact more group of spectators in genuine terms and gets itself built up with no issue.

Improved brand steadfastness

When you have a social media nearness, you make it simpler for your clients to discover you and associate with you. By associating with your clients through social media, you are progressively plausible to upsurge client maintenance and client reliability. Since building up a devoted client base is one of the primary objectives of practically any business. Consumer loyalty and brand dependability regularly go connected at the hip. It is basic to often connect with your clients and start building up a bond with them. Social media isn't simply restricted to presenting your item, it is additionally a main stage for limited time battles. A client considers these to be as administration channels where they can legitimately speak with the business.

More advantageous consumer loyalty

Social media assumes an indispensable job in systems administration and correspondence stage. With the assistance of these stages, making a voice for your organization is significant in improving the general brand picture. Clients value the way that when they post remarks on your page, they get a modified answer instead of an electronic message. A brand that qualities its clients, sets aside the effort to create an individual message, which is seen normally in a positive light.

Commercial center mindfulness

Perhaps the most ideal approaches to discover the necessities and needs of your clients rather than straightforwardly speaking with them is Marketplace mindfulness. It is additionally considered as the most significant bit of leeway of social media. By watching the exercises on your profile, you can see clients' advantage and conclusions that you probably won't know generally if you didn't have a social media nearness. As a correlative research apparatus, social media can assist you with showing signs of improvement comprehension of your industry. When you get an enormous after, you would then be able to utilize extra devices to look at different socioeconomics of your purchasers.

More brand authority

For making your business all the more dominant, brand dedication and consumer loyalty both assume a significant job, however everything comes down to correspondence. When clients see your organization posting on social media, particularly answering to their questions and posting unique substance, it causes them construct a positive picture in their brains. Routinely cooperating with your clients demonstrates that you and your business care about them. When you get a couple of fulfilled clients, who are vocal about their positive buy understanding, you can give the promoting a chance to be accomplished for you by certified clients who valued your item or administration.

Expanded traffic

One of different advantages of Social Media is that it additionally helps increment your site traffic. By sharing your substance on social media, you are giving clients motivation to navigate to your site. On your social record, the greater quality substance you share, the more inbound traffic you will produce while making change openings.

Improved SEO rankings

Social media nearness is turning into an indispensable factor in ascertaining rankings. Nowadays, to verify a fruitful positioning, SEO necessities are constantly differing. In this way, it is never again enough to just streamline your site and routinely update your blog. Businesses sharing their substance on social media are conveying a brand sign to search engine that addresses your brand legitimacy, uprightness, and consistency.

There is no denying that Social media marketing has numerous points of interest for new companies and built up brands. By standard refreshing the correct social media marketing technique, it will prompt expanded traffic, better SEO, improved brand reliability, more beneficial consumer loyalty and significantly more. Your opposition is now expanding on social media step by step, so don't give your rivals a chance to take your plausible clients. The prior you start, the quicker you see the development in your business.

CHAPTER 2
CREATE A WINNING SOCIAL MEDIA MARKETING STRATEGY

A social media marketing strategy is your course of action to manufacture mindfulness for your business and develop your following on social media. Making a social media strategy incorporates defining marketing objectives, picking the correct systems to utilize, and estimating your ideal outcomes. Your strategy guarantees social media positively affects your business.

While there are specific advances you can take to build up an effective social media strategy, executing it very well may be intense.

1. Set Your Social Media Goals

To set your social media objectives, you need to consider what you need to achieve and make an objective that is SMART (Specific, Measurable, Achievable, Relevant, and Time-bound.) Different businesses will have different objectives, so consider your alternatives and let your objectives direct the remainder of your strategy.

Here are a five general social media objectives to use as a beginning stage:

Increment brand mindfulness: This is useful for fresher businesses that are attempting to make their brand all the more outstanding through developing and connecting with a social media following.

Create new leads: If you're searching for new leads, you can utilize social media to get email endorsers, occasion registrants, and new leads.

Drive site traffic: If your business needs to build traffic to blog entries or item pages on your site, you can share interfaces on social media to drive traffic back to your webpage.

Increment online deals: If you have a web based business, you can utilize social media to run advancements and promotions to build deals.

Strengthen client care: If your business needs a focal spot to address client questions and concerns, you can utilize social media as your center point to cooperate with clients on the web.

Consider the objectives above and pick a couple of objectives that will be most useful to your business. Then make the objective more grounded by applying it straightforwardly to your business. A solid objective incorporates a number and a time span. For instance, a gems store should utilize social media to build their online deals by 20 percent in December. A marketing specialist's objective may be to drive 100 new leads in three weeks by advancing their up and coming online course on social media.

2. Figure out Which Social Media Channels Are Right for You

Picking the correct social media channels begins with understanding your intended interest group and which social systems they are well on the way to utilize. The social media channels you center around ought to likewise be appropriate to your objectives. For instance, if you are a B2B hoping to get create more leads, LinkedIn is a decent channel to concentrate on.

If you're brand new to social media, it's totally fine to concentrate on only one channel at first and grow a nearness there first. Facebook or Instagram is often the best spot to begin. As you get progressively agreeable, you might need to extend to a couple of more systems to arrive at a greater amount of your crowd if they utilize extra channels.

When choosing which channels to build up a nearness on, consider your clients and your rivals. What are your client socioeconomics? Which channels would they say they are probably going to utilize? If you need assistance delving into your intended interest group, we have a client profile format to assist you with making a careful depiction of your optimal client.

Concerning your rivals, run a Google search of their business name to check whether any social media pages spring up. Then visit your rivals' sites to check whether they have catches to any social media locales. If your rivals have followings on a social channels, you likely ought to as well.

Set aside some effort to acquaint yourself with the significant social media channels, each channel's key statistic, and what it's best for. The fundamental social media channels you have to consider are Facebook, Twitter, Instagram, LinkedIn, Pinterest, YouTube, and Snapchat.

3. Set Up Your Social Media Accounts

Presently take a couple of moments to pursue your records. This will presumably be the most effortless advance on this rundown. All significant social media channels are allowed to set up, and most make it simple directly from their landing page. A few systems, as Facebook, require an individual account before you set up a Page for your business.

Here are the connections you need:

Facebook: To make a Facebook business page, you have to make an individual profile first. Making your record is conceivable in merely seconds.

Twitter: Creating a record will require you pick a Twitter handle, however don't overthink this progression. You will have the option to refresh your handle if you need to later on.

Instagram: Download the Instagram application on your cell phone to set up your record. Select a business represent better acknowledgment and investigation.

LinkedIn: Create an individual record first so you can without much of a stretch make a Company page for your business.

Pinterest: Make sure to make a business record (or convert your own record to a business account) so you can run Pinterest advertisements later on.

YouTube: YouTube is claimed by Google, so you'll require a Google account first. Then you can visit YouTube and redo your page with your business data.

Snapchat: Download the Snapchat application on your cell phone. Note that you can't change your username on Snapchat, so utilize a handle that will be conspicuous as your business.

While these social media stages can be gotten to through an internet browser, Instagram and Snapchat are both principally portable applications. All other significant organizes likewise have portable application forms that merit downloading with the goal that you can get to your channels in a hurry.

Now, you just need to pursue your records. Try not to stress over filling in any extra data yet. There's a little research and investigation you ought to do first to ensure you're setting up your pages for progress.

4. Investigate the Competition

Prior to jumping into posting content, set aside a smidgen of effort to research your opposition and dissect their methodology. Observe what number of devotees or Likes they have, what substance they're posting, how often they're posting, and what number of Likes and Comments they're jumping by and large. Focus on how they are situating their business on social media so you can accomplish something comparative or purposefully different to stick out.

Rundown a couple of things you like about their record and a couple of things you figure you could improve. This examination can give some great motivation to how you need to move toward your social media channels and what benchmarks you can set for your very own records.

5. Manufacture Your Initial Presence

Building your underlying nearness means rounding out your business data, including a couple of pictures, and making your first post. Try not to attempt to begin fabricating an after until you have a solid establishment and you've rounded out all the fundamental data on your page. Most channels work admirably of strolling you through the important advances.

Here's a synopsis of general steps you should take:

Enter your business data: Provide an outline of your business, your contact subtleties, and a connect to your site.

Transfer pictures: You most likely need your profile picture to be something conspicuous, similar to your logo or a head shot. Ensure your pictures are the best possible sizes and show well on work area and portable perspectives.

Make your first post: Make sure individuals who land on your page get a decent initial introduction. Your first post can be something basic like: Welcome to the [business name] Facebook Page! Like our Page for [type of substance you will provide].

Pursue your contacts: Start with your most steadfast clients who you realize will Like and Follow your new record. Most social channels have prescribed contacts that make great first associations.

6. Make a Social Media Schedule

A social media timetable is a set schedule of substance thoughts to help you reliably post quality content on social media, which is critical to accomplishing your objectives and developing your following. Social media is about consistency, so in a perfect world you are committing around 15 to 20 minutes every day to social media to post and connect with your adherents consistently.

To begin, make a rundown of all the different sorts of substance you'd like to share on a progressing premise. Remember that you don't need all your substance to act naturally serving and limited time. A typical social media best practice is to pursue the 80/20 rule, which means 80 percent of your substance is helpful, instructive, or engaging and 20 percent is deals driven.

For instance, a yoga studio should post a blend of substance that incorporates inspirational statements, 30-second video tips from their teachers, connections to their week after week class plan, supportive articles, limits for new individuals, and photographs from their ongoing classes.

You don't need to post on social media consistently and it's OK to reuse some substance if you're dynamic on different channels. Be that as it may, you need to ensure each system has its own one of a kind worth and that you're connecting with clients all the time.

With 67 percent of shoppers presently utilizing social media as a client care channel, ensure you are speaking with your crowd in a convenient way. To remain over your posting timetable and approaching messages, investigate utilizing a social media the executives device to assist you with remaining sorted out and spare time. There are a ton of alternatives, incorporating apparatuses with free forms like Buffer or Hootsuite.

7. Advance Your Social Channels

Advancing your social media channels means getting the word out about your new channels so more individuals will tail you. It is the most ideal approach to develop your following with the goal that every one of your posts are seen by whatever number individuals as would be prudent. You most likely have more places to advance your social media channels than you might suspect, and a significant number of them won't cost anything to have an effect.

Here are a few places you can advance your channels:

Your site: Add catches to your social channels so site guests can without much of a stretch locate your social records.

Your email list: Once you dispatch your social records, let your email rundown know. Then, incorporate catches to your social diverts in the footer of each marketing email.

Your email signature: Add social media connects to your business email's mark.

Send an email to your staff: Encourage your staff to pursue your social media channels and welcome their group of spectators to do likewise.

In-store signage: Put up signage in your store with your social media handle or URL.

Your other social media channel: Encourage your group of spectators to tail you on different channels.

Social notices: You can run a promotion to get before new crowd individuals.

8. Measure Your Results

Your outcomes will give you how your social media endeavors are satisfying and how you're piling toward your objectives. You'll have the option to perceive what number of adherents you've picked up, how much traffic you're heading to your site, and how much commitment your posts are getting. All significant social media systems give you access to measurements however their examination stages. If you choose to utilize a social media the executives device, it will likewise likely have investigation accessible for you to utilize.

How about we audit some regular measurements that should prove to be useful:

Adherents/Likes – Shows the size of your social media group of spectators

Reach – Shows what number of individuals are really observing your social media posts

Commitment – The quantity of Likes, Comments, and Shares your substance is getting

Snaps – The occasions your posts are tapped on

If you're posting different posts seven days, you'll have a great deal of information to audit. Take a gander at your general execution on in any event a month to month premise, just as individual post execution measurements about once per week. After some time, you'll become familiar with what sort of substance drives the best results for your specific objective, which will assist you with investing energy in the things that truly drive premium and activity.

9. Enhance for the Best Performance

When you have a few information in your back pocket, you ought to have the option to apply a few learnings to your posting plan and improve for the best execution. See what's getting your business the most snaps, impressions, and commitment, and afterward change your timetable join a greater amount of these kinds of posts. For instance, if your yoga studio sees a great deal of commitment on recordings, you might need to try different things with making more recordings on channels like Facebook Live, Instagram Stories, or YouTube.

Optimization is the thing that will truly assist you with meeting and surpass your objectives. If you're experiencing difficulty getting the group of spectators development or commitment you're searching for, you may need to attempt some brand new thoughts. Perhaps it's a great opportunity to attempt a paid promotion to get before another focused on crowd. Investigate adding hashtags to your presents on increment reach. Or then again, take a stab at posting an overview or survey to ask your supporters straightforwardly what they are keen on observing from your business.

Measurements can disclose to you a great deal about how to improve your substance, yet some of the time the best optimization originates from direct one-on-one discussions with your clients. Try not to think little of the intensity of understanding your intended interest group and giving them important or engaging substance.

The Concord Cheese Shop shows they comprehend what substance reverberates with their group of spectators by posting a fun article about the advantages of red wine. The article brought about 132 responses and more than 60 offers.

10. Run Promotions for Your Products and Services

In the wake of developing your underlying after, social media advancements are an incredible method to get your items or administrations before a bigger crowd and produce a few deals. Prior to burning through cash on social media commercials, have a go at posting an opportune and convincing idea to your channels. Make certain to utilize a convincing picture to attract your crowd.

Entryway County Coffee and Tea Company works superbly with their 25th Anniversary advancement. The advancement is opportune in festivity of their commemoration. They compose clear and convincing duplicate with all the offer subtleties. In conclusion, they incorporate a brilliant picture with the rebate unmistakably included so it will bounce out to anybody looking through their feed rapidly.

Your social advancements ought to be clear, convincing, and simple to follow up on. If your deal is running over a little while, it's likewise fine to post about it more than once. Criticalness is a significant component of a fruitful advancement, so make certain to post about your deal in its most recent 24 hours.

Test advancements normally to see which offers bring about the most deals. Simply try to keep that 80/20 split, with 80 percent of your substance concentrated on offering some incentive and 20 percent limited time. That way, your group of spectators won't feel immersed with deals driven substance and they'll be all the more ready to make buys from you.

11. Run Ads on Social Media

All the significant social media stages (Facebook, Twitter, Instagram, LinkedIn, Pinterest, Snapchat, and YouTube) have social publicizing highlights to help develop your deals and crowd size. You don't really need to run social media advertisements for your business. In any case, if you are hoping to advance your item or administration to contact another crowd, social media advertisements are an incredible method to build your span. If you have an item or administration, return to the fruitful natural advancements you've run previously and consider how you can reuse the effective components of this idea in your paid advancement.

Here are a couple of different instances of social media advertisements you can run:

Storewide limits – Give your group of spectators complete opportunity to pick the item or administration they need to buy at a limited cost.

New item advancements – Drive mindfulness and deals for new items by highlighting them in a promotion.

New client bargains – Target non-clients with your social media advertisements and give them a motivating force to make a first buy with you.

Digital book downloads – Show your industry aptitude and develop your following by elevating your digital book to a focused on group of spectators.

Online class/occasion advancements – Increase participation for your on the web or disconnected occasion by elevating a welcome to your up and coming occasion.

Giveaways – Spark some enthusiasm for your business by advancing a free giveaway. You can connection to a sweepstakes presentation page, gather contact subtleties, and pick a champ.

To truly profit on most social media channels, you commonly need to burn through cash on paid advertisement battles. Paid advertisements assist you with contacting a bigger group of spectators, particularly because social media calculations limit what number of your current devotees see your natural (or free) advancements.

Every stage has its very own publicizing highlights, however there are a couple of things you can do to take advantage of your advertisements on any system:

Target Ads for Your Audience

Set up your promotion crusades so they contact a group of people that is important to your business. Every stage has its own focusing on highlights, however many enable you to target crowd individuals dependent on socioeconomics, areas, communicated intrigue, or conduct. Invest some energy refining your ideal group of spectators before distributing any notice.

Make Multiple Versions of Your Ad

With another group of spectators, it's difficult to tell what will play out the best. When running a promotion crusade, you need to make numerous renditions of your advertisement with some slight varieties. It might be least demanding to begin with two variants of an advertisement, so you can run a basic A/B test. Then, change the more fruitful promotion by testing out different offers, imaginative, and duplicate to perceive what is playing out the best.

If you need assistance making numerous rendition of your advertisement, consider finding a social media advisor on Fiverr to help make various promotion adaptations. This is the most ideal approach to test rapidly with the goal that you can perceive what kinds of duplicate, pictures, and offers will work the best.

Streamline for a Specific Metric

When you run your promotion, beware of your outcomes consistently. You will need to change your way to deal with profit on poor-performing advertisements. When improving your promotions, ensure you're concentrating on one specific measurement. Is your objective to have a huge amount of reach or to drive snaps to your site? Prior to making any progressions to your promotion, think about which advertisement renditions are helping you arrive at your ideal final product.

CHAPTER 3
CHOOSING THE RIGHT SOCIAL MEDIA PLATFORM

When you're caught up with maintaining your business, it's difficult to see time as dynamic on each social media outlet out there. Narrowing down your decision to only a chosen few platforms will enable you to center your endeavors and get the best return on your time venture.

So how would you pick the best social media platform? Here are three stages to figure out which platform is ideal for your business.

Stage 1: Identify your group of spectators

The initial step is to identify who your group of spectators is. You need to be as specific as could be allowed, since it will settle on your choice simpler. Record the responses to the accompanying inquiries:

Who is your normal client?

How old would they say they are?

Is it true that they are male or female?

What is their pay and training level?

What are they inspired by outside of your item and administration?

Utilize the responses to these inquiries (and whatever other appropriate inquiries that may identify with the business or industry you're in) so as to assist work with excursion a profile of your group of spectators.

Stage 2: Define your objectives

When you know your group of spectators, you have to characterize objectives for that crowd. As a business proprietor, your essential objective will probably be to drive deals by pulling in clients yet, there are other innovative objectives for social media. While a few brands utilize social media to drive brand acknowledgment and to grow neighborly associations with potential purchasers, others utilize social media for client care.

For instance, on-request media organization Netflix utilizes the Twitter handle @Netflixhelps to address client care issues. In addition to the fact that it frees up their telephone lines, yet it offers fulfilled clients a chance to advance their brand.

When it comes to making your social media objectives, conceptualize a rundown of both regular and strange ways social media could work for your brand.

Stage 3: Find your group of spectators

Since you have your group of spectators profiled and your objectives characterized, it's an ideal opportunity to discover your crowd. To do this, you will figure out which platform your group of spectators utilizes by taking a gander at the socioeconomics of the clients on every platform. You'll likewise need to think about how dynamic your group of spectators is on that platform. For instance, while youthful Facebook clients may have profiles, they're progressively dynamic on Instagram.

Other than socioeconomics and commitment, you'll additionally need to take a gander at how people utilize the platform.

The following is a manual for a portion of the significant social media platforms to assist you with finding your crowd.

Facebook

Facebook reports over 1.3 billion clients that is bigger than the number of inhabitants in China! With such commotion, it's essential to recollect how people use Facebook: to fabricate connections and keep contact with old companions. This makes Facebook a decent platform for building the steadfastness of your current client base.

The drawback to Facebook is that it might be difficult to contact another crowd; because of its enormous populace, your posts have a restricted reach-even inside your very own systems.

As you evaluate Facebook as a potential platform, cautiously think about your business objectives. If you're attempting to secure new business, Facebook probably won't be your best choice, yet if you're constructing a committed after of customers and you need an approach to stay in contact with them, this is an incredible choice for your business.

Twitter

Twitter is a fantastic platform to assemble mindfulness for your brand. Twitter uses the hashtag, which composes discussions around a word or expression. Via searching hashtags, you can realize what individuals are discussing so you can make your tweets to partake in well-known discussions. For what reason would you do this? Because Twitter can offer knowledge into what themes are inclining, Twitter is often utilized by news outlets to discover stories.

Since Twitter is often used to give continuous updates to a group of people, numerous brands join Twitter with disconnected commitment, for example, occasions.

Pinterest

Pinterest is utilized for "scrapbooking"□ or, as such, sparing substance by "pinning"□ photographs to a virtual notice board. Female clients rule the Pinterest statistic. Probably the most well-known pins are plans, style thoughts, striking photos, and DIY makes.

Since Pinterest is a visual-based platform, you'll need solid illustrations to draw in clients. Fruitful business utilization of Pinterest has been connected to solid retail deals.

YouTube

In spite of the fact that YouTube flaunts 1 billion clients, its range stretches out far past that. You don't need to join to be a client to view content on YouTube.

Therefore, YouTube has gotten one of the greatest search engine platforms. A significant number of these searches are for "How To"☐ recordings. Administration industry businesses who can offer this kind of substance function admirably on this platform.

LinkedIn

LinkedIn has the differentiation of being the most used platform for more seasoned spectators. It flaunts the biggest clients among ages 30-49. LinkedIn is likewise one of a kind because it has a thin core interest. Individuals use LinkedIn to search for occupations and to arrange expertly. Thus, the platform is helpful for B2B lead age, general systems administration, just as selecting workers.

Instagram

Instagram is one of the quickest developing platforms, particularly among a youthful crowd. Like Pinterest, Instagram depends on photographs for discussion. Therefore, this platform works truly well for visual based businesses, similar to craftsmanship, nourishment, retail, and excellence.

Because it's a developing platform, there's less commotion than Facebook. This implies the platform is valuable for producing leads because your scope is more extensive.

Google+

Google+ is known for a more established male statistic. This platform functions admirably for businesses in the product, engineering, and configuration spaces.

Because the platform is connected to Google Search, it conveys more weight in directing people to your site. In this way, you ought to consider the utilization of Google+ if your objective is search engine optimization.

Tips for Picking the Right Social Media Platform for Your Business

Regardless of whether you just began your business or you have a set up organization, you may be asking yourself whether you ought to be on one or the entirety of the accompanying social media platforms. Maybe your business accomplice is guiding you to make a Facebook profile, Pinterest board, Snapchat channel, and each other social platform that is accessible, possibly Vimeo.

Rather than taking on more than you can realistically handle, you need to make a stride back and think about which social platform is best for your business and will help achieve your objectives and arrive at your intended interest group. Since social platforms are free, it is enticing to believe that it is another corresponding marketing outlet that will enable you to contact a greater amount of your intended interest group; in any case, numerous ramifications accompany that choice.

Prior to building a social media strategy, you have to comprehend what your essential business goal is on social media (i.e., direct people to your site, increment adherents, assemble brand mindfulness). When you comprehend your business destinations, you can use the accompanying five hints on the most proficient method to pick which social media platform is best for your business.

1. Comprehend the motivation behind every social platform.

Before you start opening a record on each social platform, it is fundamental to comprehend what every platform does. If your intended interest group is recent college grads, being on Instagram and Snapchat may appear the correct choice. You may be correct, however it is fundamental to comprehend your group of spectators' conduct and how they will find your brand and business on social. Facebook's crucial to "Enable individuals to assemble network and unite the world." If you are a nearby business, Facebook is an extraordinary platform that enables you to interface with your neighborhood network and fabricate mindfulness around your brand.

Also, as per Pew Research, Facebook is the most generally utilized social platform. Instagram is visual; YouTube is video-based; Facebook is network building; Yelp is surveys of eateries; and Pinterest is visual motivation. When you comprehend the reason for every social platform, it will enable you to limit which platform will be best for your business. The following segment of understanding the importance of every platform is client use.

2. The numbers don't lie.

Contingent upon your business objectives, it is basic to comprehend where your crowd is and pick in like manner. For instance, if you are in the design business, Pinterest and Instagram would be the most favored platform. "93% of dynamic [Pinterest] pinners said they use Pinterest to get ready for buys," and it is mostly visual, where 81% of Pinterest clients are females. As indicated by the 2016 Pew study, "95 percent of all Instagram clients in the U.S. likewise use Facebook, trailed by Pinterest (54 percent), and Twitter (49 percent)."

Notwithstanding understanding the reason for every social platform, realizing the client's exhibition will put you on the ball. You need to be the place your devotees are. Investigate your present site traffic. If most of them are females that incline toward the visuals on each point of arrival, then Instagram, Facebook, and Pinterest are incredible platforms for your business. If you are a hardware organization, clients will depend on recordings to see how to utilize your apparatus. YouTube how-to recordings may make extraordinary, edible substance that clients will discover significant.

3. Where are your rivals?

What is your industry's focused scene? Is there a specific social influencer or brand that stands apart to you? Who's tailing them? Whom would they say they are supporting?

When searching for a social media master, you have to ensure that they do an exhaustive aggressive examination to address those inquiries. The report will help check where your rivals are and which platform would be best for your business dependent on industry. Understanding your aggressive scene will help you in building a strategy for focusing on influencers, brand envoys, and group of spectators to buy your item and recall your brand on social.

4. Consistency is critical to being essential.

You have gotten your aggressive examination report, checked the numbers, and you have picked the social media platforms that are best for your business. Before you immediately start making your records, ensure that your substance is predictable and the handle you guarantee is the equivalent over all channels. A handle is your social username. It's mistaking for your group of spectators and adherents if your social handles are for the most part different, so ensure that they are predictable over all platforms.

Next, ensure you have a business logo picture that you can transfer as your profile picture over all platforms (Remember, consistency is so significant!), particularly if you need individuals to recollect what your identity is. When transferring a profile and header picture, ensure the photographs are the correct social measurements.

5. Try not to push a similar substance on all platforms.

One of the greatest no-no's in social media marketing is cross-posting, which is pushing a similar substance on the entirety of your platforms. It looks excess and lethargic. The test with this is it requires a lot of time and intending to set up which substance ought to go on which platform, yet that leads me back to tip #1. Every platform can be used differently. Ensure that your social media master strolls you through platforms, booking recurrence, and substance strategy that will be best for meeting your business destinations.

Keep in mind, more isn't in every case better. You need to be mindful and key when picking which social platform is best for your business. Your clients and devotees are coming to you to discover significant and extraordinary substance.

By comprehension and executing the five hints above, you can advance your social marketing strategy and discover platforms that supplement and bolster your business targets. There's no free lunch. Also, in this situation the social platforms are free, however your time and business objectives are most certainly not. When you are vital and mindful about your substance on every platform, you will receive the rewards of better commitment and progressively steadfast supporters.

Quality exceeds amount, particularly on social.

CHAPTER 4
SOCIAL MEDIA ADVERTISING

While there are many different marketing strategies, just one can get predictable deals from the very first moment: social media publicizing.

Social media promoting, or social media focusing on, are notices served to clients on social media platforms. Social systems use client data to serve exceptionally important notices dependent on cooperations inside a specific platform. In numerous cases, when target market lines up with the client socioeconomics of a social platform, social publicizing can give enormous increments in changes and deals with the lower cost of securing.

What Are The Benefits Of Advertising On Social Media Channels?

For what reason is social media promoting your best publicizing wagered for fast ROI? Because...

Most channels require significant lead time to yield a ROI. For instance, content marketing works best over the long run after it has had the option to yield backlinks and SEO footing.

A few channels yield snappy results yet not all day every day. For instance, influencer marketing can gain you speedy outcomes as far as deals for low exertion (however significant expense). Be that as it may, those outcomes don't keep happening after some time. Rather, you acquire deals on a for every post premise, and often less each time it is posted.

A few channels are reliable however tedious to dial in. For instance, AdWords can deliver steady outcomes for your brand, yet it requires a significant stretch of time to ace and win specific arrangement.

With social media publicizing, you can have predictable deals rolling in from the principal day your site is live.

For present day web based business locales, the capacity to immediately and reliably acquire new clients is a HUGE arrangement. Regardless of whether you can't accomplish net positive income on the underlying deal, referrals, email marketing and client maintenance can satisfy broadly with each negligible client.

This is the reason worldwide social promotion spending multiplied from $16 billion out of 2014 to $31 billion out of 2016 and is anticipated to build another 26% in 2017.

In this guide, we will investigate how YOU can drive predictable deals for your site through social media promoting.

We'll take a gander at probably the most prevalent social platforms, give some propelled strategies and tips for dialing in your crusades, and show you how to proficiently oversee multi-channel promoting without losing your brain.

How about we begin.

The Different Types Of Social Media Platforms To Serve Ads:

Social systems administration (Facebook, LinkedIn, Google+).

Microblogging (Twitter, Tumblr).

Photograph sharing (Instagram, Snapchat, Pinterest).

Video sharing (YouTube, Facebook Live, Periscope, Vimeo).

Best Social Networks for Ecommerce Advertising
New social media systems turn out each week, the vast majority of which will never increase any kind of footing. As we would see it, it's ideal to begin with the most famous platforms, then once you have gainful frameworks running, you can take a gander at assigning a level of your financial limit toward progressively test crusades.

In 2019, there are 6 different social media channels where you can pursue demonstrated promotion strategies and produce predictable ROI.

These are the best places to contribute your advertisement cash at this moment.

Facebook.

Instagram.

Twitter.

Pinterest.

LinkedIn.

Snapchat.

Advantages Of Advertising Through Social Media Include:

Develop your deals and your fanbase.

Use client created content for promotions (which perform better, as well!).

Better target net new and returning clients (so you squander less cash).

A/B test on the fly, utilizing platform examination to decide victors.

An entrancing aspect concerning social promoting is that there is for all intents and purposes no restriction to your capacity to scale.

You don't need to trust that somebody will search for your focused on watchwords. You don't need to trust that somebody will run your advancement or read your blog. If you need to contact 50,000 individuals in a single day, you can.

Which social media arrange you pick will rely upon 3 VERY significant variables:

Where your objective clients are most focused (use, gatherings, and so forth.)

Where your objective clients are most open (favored media, promotion focusing on, and so forth.)

Where your objective clients most effectively draw in with advertisements (testing required)

Discovering accomplishment on social media expects you to string various needles together to some degree consistently.

You need to exhibit a convincing offer through a convincing medium to individuals who will really think that its convincing, in a spot those individuals will really observe it.

When you include the promoting component top of that, you additionally need to a discover a platform where clients will effectively connect with paid advertisements.

We should investigate what every one of these 6 platforms offer to enable you to choose where it merits your time and cash to contribute.

Not certain where to begin? Need some master help – for no extra cost?

Get a free social publicizing assessment today to make sense of where you should twofold down to help your arrival on advertisement spend.

1. Facebook Advertising

Facebook is THE all-inclusive social media arrange.

Within excess of 2 billion month to month clients, Facebook has over a fourth of the total populace, furnishing publicists with an unrivaled chance to reach practically anybody and everybody.

Where Facebook Advertising Shines

When it comes to online business, Facebook exceeds expectations at lead age.

If you need email addresses, Facebook is the spot to go, with numerous promoters revealing costs beneath $1 per lead.

The most widely recognized model utilized is to run a Facebook advertisement legitimately into a high-changing over point of arrival offering some assortment of a free lead magnet or group item.

Regular instances of substance for social media publicizing efforts include:

Whitepapers.

Digital books.

Item coupons.

Sitewide limits.

Restricted time offers.

Giveaways.

Free sending.

These leads would then be able to be sustained with a focused on autoresponder that acquaints them with your brand and items.

Numerous online business brands likewise use packaged item contributions to commute home apparent esteem and acquire immediate transformation.

Facebook permits further developed focusing than some other promoting platform on earth. Sponsors can focus by area (inside a 5-mile range), set of working responsibilities, interests, past action, and numerous other staggeringly significant criteria.

How Facebook Advertising is Priced

Valuing changes generally dependent on a few components, including the group of spectators you're attempting to target and the spending you set for your promotions.

When in doubt, the more cash you spend, the more effective Facebook's calculation becomes at spending your cash, expanding your advertisement execution after some time.

As per a broad investigation was done by Ad Espresso, the normal cost per click (CPC) of Facebook promotions starting at 2016 was about .28 pennies and the cost per 1,000 impressions (CPM) was $7.19.

The examination proceeded to separate it by age and sex too. The 65+ age assembled demonstrated the most constant pattern of lower CPC costs after some time. Females cost by and large 4 pennies more prominent CPC than focusing on guys.

Step by step instructions to Set Up Facebook Advertising Campaigns

There are 3 center parts to setting fully operational effective Facebook advertisement battles:

Setting up your promotion

Setting up focusing on

Setting up retargeting

For a bit by bit guide covering the initial 2 sections, look at this guide from Neil Patel. For a how-to manual for setting up retargeting, pursue this guide from Conversion Sciences.

Facebook Advertising Advanced Tactics

Try not to run the equivalent accurate ad(s) to the entirety of your crowds. Your prospecting and retargeting advertisements ought to be exceptional, and your promotions for every group of spectators "intrigue" section ought to be custom-fitted to that crowd.

Use prospecting advertisements to assemble brand mindfulness and show individuals your item, and afterward use retargeting promotions to take care of business with clients who have just flagged intrigue. Retargeting promotions are perfect for a forceful pitch and close.

The utilization of emoticons in promotions has been fanning out quickly, even among bigger, progressively settled brands. They can be exceptionally effective at driving higher CTRs, however similarly as with all strategies, you should A/B test for yourself no doubt.

Continuously be trying! Promotion weariness is an ever-present test on Facebook, and it's ideal to pivot in and test new advertisements at regular intervals.

Copy crowds are a staple for some promoters... and which is all well and good. They will in general work very well for prospecting. So, you should take care not to layer extra focusing over the carbon copies if you can maintain a strategic distance from it. You risk contracting your potential reach and passing up important clients.

Better Facebook Advertising Results in 5 Minutes

Big Commerce clients utilizing Ecommerce Insights can rapidly send out a rundown of their most elevated AOV and most elevated LTV client partners and afterward utilize those to discover carbon copies on Facebook.

Takes 5 minutes.

See Facebook Advertising in real life

An extraordinary case of Facebook promotions in real life originates from Spearmint LOVE, a child garments brand out of Arizona.

The author's better half, John Lott, spent a whole year attempting to nail down the brand's Facebook retargeting effort. Through spreadsheets and following and change pixels back on the site, his diligent work satisfied.

His mystery? Accomplices matter – a ton.

"Following 3 years of building a group of people and extraordinary associations with our item accomplices, we realized the time had come to perceive how rapidly we could develop the business," says John Lott, CFO/COO, Spearmint LOVE. "Our initial Facebook promotions were finished distinct advantages for us. In 2016, we became 1110% more than 2015, energized for the most part by Facebook promotions. Facebook publicizing keeps on being the foundation of our promotion strategy."

Spearmint LOVE has been so fruitful with Facebook promoting, truth be told, that Sheryl Sandberg, COO at Facebook, posted about them after Facebook's Q2 2017 quarterly report.

2. Instagram Advertising

While Facebook's amazing client numbers make it the undisputed lord of social media, the organization's most blazing procurement is starting to resemble the ruler of social publicizing.

Instagram now flaunts in excess of 500 million month to month dynamic clients and directions one of the most elevated crowd commitment rates in social media, 58% higher than Facebook and 2000% higher than Twitter.

Instagram's commitment rates are 58% higher than Facebook's and 2,000% higher than Twitter's.

Where Instagram Advertising Shines

Instagram is, obviously, very picture and video overwhelming. All things considered, venders of items that are outwardly engaging or who can join visual media into their battles will in general perform best on this social media channel.

It is additionally important that Instagram's client base slants vigorously to the 18-29 territory and somewhat more toward females and minorities.

If any or those attributes are in arrangement with your intended interest group or purchaser persona, than chances are, Instagram will be the best advertisement decision for your business.

Not at all like natural posts, Instagram advertisements can be made to connect straightforwardly to an item page or other point of arrival, taking into consideration direct commitment with your items.

How Instagram Advertising is Priced

All things considered, Instagram promoting costs are in a similar ballpark as Facebook advertisements at a cost of $5 per thousand impressions (CPM). While the cost might be comparative, most current insights show that Instagram gets substantially more commitment on their posts and promotions than Facebook does.

For example, Victoria's Secret saw a normal of 2,078 preferences for every post on Facebook versus 283,030 on Instagram. Comparative differences have been found with brands like Mercedes Benz, McDonalds and PlayStation.

Step by step instructions to Set Up An Instagram Advertising Campaign

With Instagram being claimed by Facebook, setting up Instagram advertisements is fundamentally the same as setting up Facebook promotions. Here's a visual, bit by bit manual for propelling a battle.

Instagram Advertising Advanced Tactics

Concentrate first on custom spectators. This could be crowds made through pixel following, an email list, a supporters rundown or some other strategy. Arrangements of clients who have connected with you in the past perform best.

When you are prepared to grow past custom crowds, copy spectators ought to be your next stop. Facebook/Instagram's calculation is truly adept at finding comparative crowds that will react well to your advertisements.

Utilize custom pictures of genuine individuals. Stock photographs don't chip away at Instagram.

Make your offers powerful. Instagram's visual nature takes motivation purchasing to the following level, yet you won't take advantage of that if you aren't offering something convincing.

Pay attention to hashtags. They are somewhat of a joke wherever else, yet Instagram is driven by hashtags, and they are an extraordinary method to interface with specialty crowds.

See Instagram Ads in real life

An incredible case of Instagram promotions in real life again originates from Spearmint LOVE, demonstrating that you don't need to twofold down in just a solitary channel.

The Spearmint LOVE group had incredible accomplishment with its natural posts on Instagram, however the business truly developed in the wake of publicizing on Instagram and Facebook. To proceed with that development, the organization utilized Ads Manager to coordinate the Facebook pixel with Big Commerce, its outsider internet business site—all without contacting a solitary line of code.

For its Thanksgiving retargeting effort, the Spearmint LOVE group streamlined its advertisements for changes, and utilized information from the Facebook pixel to set up a custom crowd to retarget. The group used to physically work out its focusing on records, yet with the recently incorporated pixel, it can now consequently construct a custom crowd dependent on the individuals who visited its site inside the most recent 60 days yet didn't buy. This group of spectators is always and consequently recharged dependent on the 60-day window.

Spearmint LOVE then utilized unique advertisements, which draw from the organization's item inventory, to urge individuals to return to the site and make a buy.

Since incorporating the pixel, Spearmint LOVE has seen a 33.8X profit for promotion spend on Instagram alone and a 47% reduction in the cost per buy.

3. Twitter Advertising

Twitter has changed breaking news and given unrivaled access to clients to associate with both specialty and standard influencers.

With 328 million month to month dynamic clients, it stays one of the most well-known social media platforms.

Where Twitter Advertising Shines

All things considered, it isn't generally Twitter publicizing that sparkles...

Not at all like Facebook, Twitter is as yet a reasonable system for natural commitment. Brands don't have to pay so as to arrive at their adherents, which upgrades the platform's worth in any event, when running paid advertisements.

Overall, Twitter clients shop online 6.9x every month, while non-clients shop online simply 4.3x per month. Furthermore, there's especially uplifting news for smaller businesses: Twitter reports that 60% of clients buy from a SMB.

Internet business stores today use Twitter advertisements fundamentally to drive brand mindfulness and advance specific items for direct changes. The most well-known model is Twitter site cards facilitating under 100 characters and showing some assortment of rich media.

How Twitter Advertising is Priced

By and large, a thousand advertisement impressions (CPM) on Twitter promotions cost somewhere in the range of $9 and $11 while snaps cost around 25-30 pennies each. Both advanced crusades achieve comparable degrees of commitment at an infinitesimal cost difference.

Twitter promotion cost has been relentlessly expanding throughout the most recent 2 years because of more advertisers gradually exploiting the platform, however generally speaking, the platform is viewed as moderately underutilized for publicizing.

Twitter is viewed as moderately underutilized for promoting.

The most effective method to Set Up a Twitter Advertising Campaign

There are various different crusade types you can set up in Twitter:

Advanced Accounts

Advanced Tweets

Advanced Trends

Site Cards

For a bit by bit manual for setting up your Twitter crusades, look at this piece by KISS metrics.

Twitter Advertising Advanced Tactics

Utilize an applicable, convincing picture that offers setting to the watcher, accommodates your brand and draws consideration. Rich media is a non-debatable on Twitter.

Be very focused with the items or lead magnets you advance. Twitter requires a more engaged methodology than different channels.

Utilize a "Shop now" CTA to coordinate hotter leads back to an internet business webpage. Once more, be certain this is taking them to the specifically promoted item page or the publicized rebate or other lead magnet offer.

Incorporate client commitment legitimately with the promotion. Twitter exceeds expectations at direct association among brands and buyers. Exploit that in your advertisement battles.

Organize quickness: in the promotion, presentation page, offer duplicate, and so on., Twitter is about curtness.

See Twitter Advertising in real life

An incredible case of Twitter promotions in real life originates from Rock Tape, a gear and athletic tape retailer.

"A site snaps or changes battle enables you to utilize a Website Card with your advanced tweets. Site Cards offer a decision of source of inspiration (CTA) catches, a picture and a feature to give you a chance to direct people to your site straightforwardly from a tweet.

Advanced tweets with Website Cards drive 43% more commitment than simply tweeting out a connection.

You'll pay for snaps to your site, and you can set up online change following to see each dollar spent. You can likewise set up remarketing dependent on individuals who have just visited your site."

Rock Tape utilized this social media strategy to build commitment with their very own battles, driving clients straightforwardly to their store and expanding deals.

4. Pinterest Advertising

Pinterest is one of a kind. It's visual, as Instagram, yet dissimilar to Instagram, it is profoundly focused toward ladies with a 81% female client base.

With 175 million month to month clients, it's additionally a staggeringly dynamic platform.

Where Pinterest Advertising Shines

Pinterest is broadly viewed as a solid platform for internet business deals.

Commitment is high.

Pictures are often worked around custom item creation.

Clients deliberately utilize the platform to discover and buy innovative items.

Advanced pins mix into the Pinterest sheets and don't divert or put off would-be Pinterest clients like some different platforms do. Pinterest's socioeconomics propose items focused toward millennial ladies from the U.S. will do very well with their promotion platform, and contextual analysis information affirms this.

Online business retailers especially love the estimation of Pinterest's exceptionally focused on search engine and use Pinterest advertisements to advance their brand and items.

This procedure is cultivated by picking a high performing pin and advancing it dependent on commitment or visits to your store.

The advanced pins are then set in increasingly significant situations over Pinterest's sheets and are exceptionally obvious to those perusing and searching for catchphrases related with your brand or related things.

How Pinterest Advertising is Priced

Publicizing information is more difficult to discover with Pinterest. In the relatively recent past, promotions were over the top expensive at $30-40 for each 1,000 impressions and just accessible to huge brands.

Later reports show that clients are encountering increasingly moderate rates, with one client referring to a CPM of $5.30 and a CPC of $1.52, which would put Pinterest in a comparative ballpark to different platforms.

The most effective method to Set Up A Pinterest Advertising Campaign

When you talk about Pinterest publicizing, you are extremely simply discussing advanced pins. For a bit by bit manual for setting up your own advanced pins, look at this guide from Social Media Examiner.

Pinterest Advertising Advanced Tactics

Innovativeness sells. Clients are glancing through several pins in fast progression. If you need to get saw, you have to stick out, either through unadulterated inventiveness or imaginative eye catching.

Concentrate on patterns. What are contenders posting? What searches are drifting? What items are hot?

Draw in with your supporters. Repine your fans and use curated repines to extend your group of spectators and tap into bigger crowds.

Be point by point. Pinterest is basically a search engine. Incorporate since quite a while ago, nitty gritty depictions with watchwords and hashtags.

Be deliberate about where your pins are connecting. The navigate goal will decide if you squander the snap or transform it into a lead or deal.

See Pinterest Advertising in real life

An extraordinary case of Pinterest promotions in real life originates from Native Union, a prevalent mobile phone frill brand.

The organization reposts its high-class lifestyle pictures utilizing its items to exceptionally sort out any advanced home. The posts have helped Native Union gain discount situation in block and-mortars like Paper Source – because of their prevalence with 18-30 yr elderly people ladies.

5. LinkedIn Advertising

LinkedIn is another interesting social platform that spins basically around the B2B advertise.

LinkedIn has an expected 227 million month to month dynamic clients, uniformly split among male and female clients. 61% of clients fall into the 30-64 age range section.

Where LinkedIn Advertising Shines

LinkedIn is the place you will in general locate the most elevated normal discretionary cashflow, with 75% of LinkedIn clients gaining $50,000 every year or more. It's likewise where you will in general locate the best leads, especially in specific businesses.

In contrast to most social platforms, which exceed expectations at B2C publicizing, LinkedIn is remarkably appropriate for B2B promotions and social media marketing efforts.

Administration businesses and B2B item businesses will in general have unquestionably more accomplishment on LinkedIn than B2C retailers.

Truth be told, the ventures that see the best accomplishment with LinkedIn promoting incorporate spotters, optional training, and top of the line B2B items and administrations.

How LinkedIn Advertising is Priced

On LinkedIn, normal cost per click (CPC) ranges from $2-$7 per click and can go as high as $11 or $12.

The most effective method to Set Up A LinkedIn Advertising Campaign

There are three sorts of LinkedIn promotions:

Supported content

Supported InMail

Content advertisements

For a bit by bit manual for setting up these battles, track with this guide.

LinkedIn Advertising Advanced Tactics

Track advertisement execution strictly and dispose of any promotions performing at under a 0.10% active visitor clicking percentage (CTR). If you hit near 1% or above, scale!

While LinkedIn's advertisement focusing on might appear to be adolescent alongside Facebook, the capacity to focus by organization, organization size, titles, area, status, age, instruction and aptitudes can be unimaginably effective for B2B purposes. Use it!

LinkedIn clients incline toward shorter, pithier advertisement duplicate than their Facebook partners.

Concentrate on proficient issues and difficulties. Everybody is attempting to excel. Would you be able to support them?

A significant part of the estimation of LinkedIn lies in its gatherings. Search for approaches to arrive at those gatherings with your promotions and advertisement crusades.

See LinkedIn Advertising in real life

An incredible case of LinkedIn promotions in real life originates from Baume and Mercier, a Swiss extravagance watchmaker that has been related with creative, reasonable greatness for over 180 years.

The brand needed to contact a group of people of yearning, youthful experts crosswise over Europe and broaden mindfulness and commitment past their current client base. To do that, they looked to LinkedIn.

Utilizing a Sponsored InMail battle customized for crowds in Italy, France, Spain and the UK, the brand welcomed youthful experts to praise snapshots of achievement through locally significant encounters LinkedIn's focused on centered around the spectators with the best potential for the brand: watch darlings, youthful affluent and youthful experts advancing their professions.

Results were awesome.

The LinkedIn crusade conveyed a reaction pace of over half. 216 of those reacting proceeded to go to the occasions, with 157 giving contact subtleties. Navigate rates came in at up to 4x the benchmark, with up to 15% of those accepting InMails proceeding to go to the occasions.

Moreover, the brand became their CRM database by 1,200 new individuals, who selected in for progressing commitment with Baume and Mercier.

6. Snapchat Advertising

Snapchat is one of the more up to date platforms to develop on the scene as a focused power with 301 million month to month dynamic clients.

While it is not yet clear if the organization will capitulate to Instagram's social video push, starting at now, it's a reasonable publicizing platform with an exceptionally dynamic client base.

Where Snapchat Advertising Shines

There's extremely only one detail you have to know to comprehend the estimation of Snapchat. On some random day, Snapchat arrives at 41% of every one of the 18-multi year-olds in the United States.

... we should rehash that.

41% of ALL 18-multi year old's in the U.S. will communicate with Snapchat today.

That is the place Snapchat sparkles. However, things get dubious when it comes to evaluating...

How Snapchat Advertising is Priced + See It In Action

Snapchat has various promoting choices, the vast majority of which are very costly. Wallaroo Media furnishes us with the full breakdown:

1. Snap Ads

Snap promotions are portable, intelligent video advertisements with 5X higher swipe-up rate than the normal active visitor clicking percentage for other tantamount social platforms. These cost between $1,000 – $3,000 every month to run.

Ways To Manage Social Advertising Campaigns

Since we've investigated our top social advertisement platforms (and maybe chose 1 or 2 to seek after) it's a great opportunity to choose how to deal with our crusades.

There are three essential approaches to oversee social media crusades.

Run your promotion crusades physically

Run your promotion crusades by means of robotized programming

Contract an oversaw administration to run your promotion crusades

In all honesty, there is no "right" answer here. Each of these have qualities and shortcomings and can work for different businesses.

1. Run Your Ad Campaigns Manually

The least expensive approach to deal with your promotion crusades regarding working cost is to just run them yourself. There are no exceptional prerequisites to physically run a crusade. Simply head to the platform you wish to publicize on and set up your crusade on their site.

The Pros

On the in addition to side, running efforts yourself enables you to give 100% of your financial limit toward testing different promotions and discovering champs. Each dollar goes legitimately into genuine promoting.

Moreover, running promotions yourself will bring about you building up your own aptitude, which can be utilized to all the more likely advance your advertisements and will endure into what's to come. Regardless of whether you change strategies not far off, you will have a gauge comprehension of how publicizing on a given platform functions and a limit to quantify outside procures against.

The Cons

On the negative side, skill isn't grown medium-term, and consistently you spend acing publicizing is an hour you don't spend somewhere else. If you are a business proprietor or marketing supervisor, there is a genuinely significant open door cost on your time, and you most likely can't bear to commit the necessary hours to learn and ace social media publicizing.

Mastery isn't grown medium-term, and consistently you spend acing publicizing is an hour you don't spend somewhere else.

Furthermore, committing 100+ hours is no assurance that you will succeed, and regardless of whether you do, all things considered, your hourly rate x 100 is significantly more costly than contracting an outside support of get possibly ensured outcomes. Basically, you may be taking a huge bet with ensured drawbacks and just theoretical upsides.

Who It's Ideal For

If you don't have cash close by to contract an outside help... you don't have cash close by to procure an outside assistance. That is only your world, and it implies that if you need to run social promotions, you'll have to do it without anyone else's help.

If you are eager to get the show on the road to commit a significant measure of time to acing publicizing on a given social media channel, this can be an incredible alternative for you. If you succeed, you will have the way to acquire salary for your business uncertainly.

If you don't have the cash and don't have the opportunity, there is another alternative that may be directly for you...

CHAPTER 5
HOW SOCIAL MEDIA PLATFORM IMPROVES YOUR BUSINESS

Most small businesses are cautious about what kind of marketing strategies they put resources into. When you have a restricted marketing spending plan, it's significant that you spend it astutely to maximize your cash. Marketing through social media is one of the most adaptable and cost-effective strategies that small businesses can use to arrive at their intended interest group and lift deals after some time. That is the reason 97% of advertisers are utilizing social media to contact their crowds.

So what's so extraordinary about social media marketing? Here are our organization's best 15 reasons why marketing through social media is an unquestionable requirement for small businesses.

1. Your clients are on social media.

Probably the best purpose behind your small business to showcase through social media is that your clients are investing energy in these channels. As per Statista, 70% of the U.S. populace has in any event one social media profile. Furthermore, by 2021, the quantity of overall social media clients is required to reach about 3.1 billion individuals. With such huge numbers of customers utilizing social media consistently, this shows an extraordinary open door for small businesses who need to contact their online group of spectators.

Not exclusively are your clients on social media, however there's a decent possibility that a considerable lot of them are checking these locales consistently.

Interfacing with your intended interest group can be simple if you are dynamic on the channels that they utilize regularly. As such, don't make your group of spectators come to you – go to your crowd! If you aren't now on social media, you could be passing up a significant opportunity to associate with your clients and connect new leads.

2. Shoppers will be increasingly open to your messages when marketing through social media.

Clients are dynamic on social media platforms because these channels offer a fun and simple approach to organize, stay in contact with loved ones, and remain associated with what's happening on the planet. Normally, clients are not on these channels with the desire that they will be promoted to. Be that as it may, this doesn't imply that social media clients aren't following and collaborating with their preferred brands.

Truth be told, as indicated by Marketing Sherpa, 95% of online grown-ups ages 18 to 34 are probably going to pursue a brand on social media. Notwithstanding, when clients pursue brands and draw in with their social media profiles, it is because they locate the substance and data in these social media crusades important. Regardless of whether they are searching for bargains, appreciate engaging substance, or simply need to become familiar with the brand, social media clients are available to drawing in with brands on social media channels.

The motivation behind why purchasers might be increasingly responsive to your brand message on social media is because social media enables you to be progressively conversational and show a different side of your brand. The substance that you distribute on these channels add to your brand character and assist you with exhibiting your brand voice. On social media, you can make authentic associations with your leads and clients, as opposed to simply conveying direct marketing messages. This is something that customers are commonly increasingly receptive to.

It's presumably not different to you to discover clients and organizations examining an issue/worry about their brand on Twitter. Or on the other hand possibly you have discovered a few brands' Q and As on Instagram Stories. Most advertisers see these social media channels as an approach to become acquainted with their group of spectators better in a progressively close to home way. So you ought to as well.

3. Marketing through social media can assist increment with branding acknowledgment.

Another advantage of marketing through social media is that it causes you improve perceivability, and along these lines increment acknowledgment for your brand. Your business social media profiles present new chances to share your substance and truly present your brand's voice and character. By posting convincing substance that includes an incentive for your intended interest group, you are making your brand both increasingly available and commonplace for new leads and current clients.

For instance, suppose that another lead unearths your brand on social media. They might not have known about your organization previously, however through your social media content, they can become familiar with your brand and the worth that you give. This equivalent circumstance can apply to your present clients. Subsequent to seeing your social media content on numerous systems, existing clients can turn out to be better familiar with your business, which may build their enthusiasm for a rehash buy.

4. Marketing through social media builds your inbound traffic.

Your social media profiles give one more approach to get increasingly inbound traffic to your site. This makes marketing through social media a brilliant strategy to supplement your search engine optimization endeavors. Each bit of substance that you post to your social media profiles is another chance to carry new guests to your site. When the guest gets to your site, you will have the chance to change over.

So as to get the most inbound traffic conceivable, it's significant that you reliably distribute content that is connecting with and includes an incentive for your intended interest group. The greater quality substance that you post on your social media channels, the more open doors you need to connect new leads and direct them back to your site. If your site is advanced for transformations than it might involve time before these new leads convert into clients.

5. Different social media channels assist you with arriving at specific crowds.

Another advantage of social media marketing is that you can deliberately target different crowds dependent on the channels that your brand is dynamic on. Instead of simply putting your marketing message out there for the viewing pleasure of anyone passing by, you can arrive at your objective market and work to drive increasingly qualified leads back to your site.

Make a reasonable rundown of your crowd statistic esteems – the more point by point it is, the better. This rundown can incorporate their sexual orientation, age, area, interests, the brands they pursue, leisure activities, and so forth. Realizing these qualities will give you more thought on which social media channel you should use to contact them. Likewise, this will help you in making content that will connect with your group of spectators in this manner expanding your odds for changes. The more significant this traffic is, the more probable you will be to help change rates.

Regardless of who you are attempting to reach, you can discover your crowd on one of the numerous well known social media channels that customers are utilizing each day.

The way to taking advantage of your social media marketing is to deliberately pick which channels you intend to contribute your time, cash, and exertion in. Not certain which social media channels are directly for you? Look at our post on the best social media platforms for your business to discover increasingly about each channel and how it can profit you dependent on your intended interest group and objectives.

6. Social media promoting enables you to target and retarget perfect customers.

In spite of the fact that social media promoting requires a touch of an in advance speculation, social advertisements can do a great deal to supplement the natural crusades that you are running on your social media channels. With modern focusing on capacities, social media platforms like Facebook assist you with focusing on your optimal purchasers, which enables you to drive increasingly pertinent traffic to your site. This is the most ideal approach to take advantage of your marketing spend.

With Facebook advertisements, you can identify new potential leads by characterizing your optimal client through the promotions platform. Then, Facebook enables you to serve your promotion substance to the individuals who show similar kinds of practices that your intended interest group does. As you drive increasingly pertinent traffic to your brand site, you can improve results, regardless of what your promotion objectives might be.

7. Marketing through social media is cost effective.

Probably the best advantage of marketing through social media is that it encourages you cut marketing costs without sacrificing results. The greater part of your social media results will originate from putting time in making and distributing content just as having discussions with your fans and adherents. Fortunately even only a couple of hours seven days can have significant outcomes. Truth be told, HubSpot reports that 84% of advertisers had the option to produce expanded traffic with as meager as six hours of exertion spent on social media every week.

Regardless of whether you choose to make social media promoting a significant piece of your social media strategy, you will even now locate that social media marketing is cost effective. Contingent upon your objectives and the extent of your battle, it is moderately reasonable to run paid advertisements on social media channels like Facebook and Twitter. Regardless of how small your financial limit is, you are still ready to have an effect on these channels to reach and change over new leads.

8. Social media marketing may help improve your search engine rankings.

There's a decent possibility that you're now centered around improving your search engine optimization. Yet, did you realize that search engines might be utilizing your social media nearness as a factor in their rankings? Effective brands will in general have a solid social media nearness, so a solid social media nearness may go about as a sign to search engines that your brand is significant, valid, and reliable. In spite of the fact that the positioning components are continually changing, it's almost certain that dynamic social media channels will wind up helping you at last.

Search engines focus on your social media conduct, particularly connections to social substance and social sign like likes and offers.

Not exclusively could your social media nearness sway your search engine rankings, however it's essential to take note of that your social media profiles will in all probability appear on the principal page of Google when purchasers are searching for your brand. If the purchaser taps on your social profiles and finds that they are obsolete or unengaging, they may choose to take their business somewhere else. That is the reason it's imperative to not just reliably distribute convincing substance on your social media channels, yet in addition check your profile data occasionally and make changes and updates as required.

9. Your opposition is on social media.

Regardless of what industry you are in or who your objective market is, there is a decent possibility that your rivals are as of now present and included on social media channels. This not just proposes that there is open door for your brand to do well on these channels, however it implies that a portion of your potential clients may as of now be conversing with the challenge at this very moment.

If you need to stay focused in the computerized commercial center, it's essential that you start moving in the direction of building a nearness on social media. Social media substance enables you to not just show a smidgen of your brand character, however it additionally introduces an effective outlet for exhibiting your industry ability and information. This is probably the most ideal approaches to separate yourself from the challenge and acquire progressively pertinent online traffic.

10. Marketing on social media prompts higher change rates.

As indicated by HubSpot, social media has a 100% higher lead-to-close rate than outbound marketing strategies. That could be because each post you make and every communication you have on your social media channels is a chance to change over an intrigued lead into a glad client. By building a report with your leads and clients and posting significant substance consistently, your brand can work to improve trust and believability, which prompts more transformations.

The most significant component of social media that outcomes in more changes is the capacity to carry an increasingly human part to your brand informing. Since social media is a spot for purchasers to socialize and organize, brands can show the human side of their brand through light, often conversational substance that enables each organization to show their character, diversion, and warmth.

11. Social media marketing improves brand unwaveringness.

While bigger organizations can bear to fabricate huge and costly client dependability programs, small businesses need to depend on other, progressively reasonable techniques for building brand devotion. Social media is an effective method to fabricate associations with leads and clients that lead to more noteworthy fulfillment and dedication after some time. Truth be told, an investigation from Texas Tech University shows that brands who connect with their present clients and target group of spectators on social media channels appreciate higher reliability from their clients.

Connecting with your clients and leads on social media causes you construct more grounded client connections. This can separate you from your opposition by indicating your group of spectators how your brand is different and fortifying that your business thinks about its clients. By connecting with your group of spectators through significant, convincing substance and discussion, you can work to transform upbeat clients into brand advocates.

12. Purchasers are searching for suggestions on social media.

Verbal marketing is one of the most incredible assets that any organization has in their marketing tool stash. In addition to the fact that it is free, it goes far in helping you manufacture trust with new leads. From numerous points of view, social media has become the new outlet for informal marketing. Presently like never before, brands are urging their clients to leave surveys on their social media profiles, prescribe their brand to loved ones on social, or give tributes.

What's more, all things considered! Customers are bound to purchase from brands that have been suggested. These proposals don't really need to originate from a companion, relative, or associate. As should be obvious by the measurements underneath, shoppers are similarly prone to believe online audits as they are to confide in close to home proposals.

In addition to the fact that consumers trust surveys on social media, however they often search them out before settling on an acquiring choice.

These measurements additionally propose that shoppers are effectively looking for suggestions on social media and that these proposals do affect their purchasing conduct. Therefore, it's significant that you effectively urge your glad clients to leave your brand an audit on social media and prescribe your items and administrations to other people. This is an incredible method to create a portion of that important verbal enchantment that enables deals to take off.

13. Social media interfaces your brand with clients you didn't know existed.

Most brands depend on search engine optimization and PPC advertisement traffic to discover and connect new leads. Notwithstanding, marketing through social media can be an incredible outlet for getting new customers. As we talked about above, suggestions or audits on social media can go far in helping your brand associate with clients that you didn't know existed. In any case, there are different ways that your organization can utilize social media to take advantage of new markets.

One way that you can discover new clients and market openings on your social channels is through social tuning in. By following certain watchwords and looking at inclining themes in your industry, you can see who is participating in the discussion. This can furnish your business with an abundance of new lead openings while additionally acquainting you with industry influencers who you might have the option to join forces with to help perceivability.

14. Marketing through social media can assist you with improving brand authority.

Marketing through social media encourages you fabricate expert for your brand. This is a significant piece of effectively situating your business as a pioneer in the commercial center. The more significant substance you are sharing on social media, the more you open doors you need to show your ability to leads and clients.

When others share your substance with their fans and devotees or notice your brand in their posts, this helps fabricate your brand authority much further. The more that social media clients talk about your brand, the more important your brand will appear to other people. This will motivate new group of spectators individuals to perceive what your business is about and even pursue your organization for your updates and bits of knowledge.

15. Social media marketing offers you the chance to increase new client bits of knowledge.

What's more, to wrap things up... social media marketing gives you the important chance to increase new bits of knowledge into your clients. By cooperating with leads and current clients on social media, you can perceive what your clients are keen on and what drives them.

If you occasionally investigate what your clients are discussing on social media, you can have a superior comprehension of what they care about most. For example, through social tuning in, you can discover what your clients most prominent difficulties and concerns are and afterward work to make increasingly content around these points. You can likewise utilize social tuning in to perceive what clients are stating about your brand specifically, and afterward utilize this data to make changes to improve consumer loyalty.

Social media likewise enables you to all the more likely comprehend what your clients' online practices resemble. For instance, you may utilize the investigation platform on Facebook to see which kinds of substance are most famous inside your objective market. You can likewise quantify your changes for posts and promotions crosswise over channels to see which battles are functioning admirably and which need somewhat more work.

CHAPTER 6
MISTAKES YOU MUST AVOID

Social media is extraordinary. Truth be told, it's great to such an extent that businesses and individuals the same use it for a large number of reasons, regardless of whether that is creating new business, making companions or setting up a notoriety dependent on straightforwardness, devotion and great good old skill (generally alluded to as substance).

In any case, social media is a major and frightening spot (it's been anticipated that by 2016, Facebook will be the biggest nation on earth), and if you're regularly going to get yourself or your business the credit it merits, then there are a couple of things that you should mind your own business. Presently before I let you know precisely what you ought to do on social media, here are a couple of things you ought to maintain a strategic distance from.

Here's 5 of those things that you shouldn't share on social media:

Recoil commendable photographs. Extravagant being an idea chief? what's more, I don't mean one of those self-titled ones... Then recollect, photographs aren't generally for sharing. If you were as of late gotten on camera embracing a lamppost or a can, your potential customers and new managers don't have to see that. Keep in mind, an image says a thousand words, and an image of you sat on the can, or eyebrows shaved and whipped cream wherever unquestionably says a ton. What's more, that is anything but something worth being thankful for.

Your own telephone number: Give out your business line, your email address, however your own cell phone number? Damnation no. Spare that for companions and family members. Keep in mind, the web is an unnerving spot, loaded with stalkers, and much more terrible... salesmen. Try not to leave your Facebook page open to spammers and cold guests around the world.

Your step by step area. Joined with refreshing the whole web on the entirety of your best in class buys, you are setting yourself up to lose. For sure. Your 32,000 or 421 supporters on Twitter don't have to know your whereabouts consistently. It'd be simpler to post a photograph of yourself with a sign saying 'ransack me please' and a rundown of your assets and address underneath.

Bank and Mastercard subtleties. If it's not too much trouble I ask of you, don't share a photo of your chic dark charge card, or the one shrouded in doggies, anyway much you like it, it simply is definitely not a keen move. You are leaving yourself open to data fraud, and great good old burglary. With wholesale fraud figures remaining at 4 million per year for the UK alone, it's sheltered to state that sharing photographs of your bank card resembles giving a canine a bone.

Stripped selfies. Nothing more needs to be said.

As yet perusing? Phew. Fingers crossed that you haven't been doing the epic blunders referenced above, however if you have, presently's the ideal opportunity for a reevaluate. What's more, if your way to deal with social media has been to offer it to the assistant, then the entirety of that is going to change.

Things you ought to do

Make solid social profiles. Extravagant yourself as a business chief of things to come? Well chip away at your online notoriety. Set up yourself in the best places, and ensure your profile is first class. That implies, no photographs taken while out at a bar, fill in each area and truly make the most out of the stunning open doors that can be found through LinkedIn and Twitter. With half of individuals getting a new line of work through systems administration and individual associations, it's anything but difficult to see the open doors that are out there on the social web.

Utilize substance to make new business. They state quality written substance is the final deciding factor, and while I may not concur with that... (read my opinion of the new King of the advanced waves, Lifecycle Marketing) I do accept that substance ought to be a fundamental piece of each advertiser and businesses social media plan. With B2B organizations that blog producing 67% a larger number of leads every month than the individuals who don't, it's unmistakable: content is huge.

Draw in with your possibilities and current clients. So your group of spectators hangs out on Twitter? Go meet them there. Or on the other hand would LinkedIn gatherings work better for you? Whatever your crowd, you can discover them on the web, and by doing your research, you can effectively target where you invest your energy on the web and improve your odds of producing new business leads. The initial step for this is understanding your customer personas, no thought what I mean? Peruse increasingly about personas here.

Look at your rivals. What's going on with they? Regardless of whether you're contemplating yourself or your business, it will profit you to see precisely what your rivals are doing and where.

5. Build up a strategy. Neglecting to design, is intending to fall flat and without knowing your ultimate objectives, how are you regularly going to arrive? Regardless of whether you are expecting to advance yourself or your business, it's critical to ask yourself what you'd like to accomplish and how you intend to accomplish it. Set up together an arrangement and use it.

Presently recall, it's a major world out there on the social web and once it's on the web, there's no halting it. Take a gander at Beyonce, her marketing expert probably battled to get those unflattering Super Bowl photographs expelled from the web, however they became famous online. Actually, who hasn't seen them? If you haven't, here's a connection...

My point is this, when it's out there, it's out there and it's essentially difficult to take it back. So think shrewdly, what amount do you esteem your notoriety, business or individual? Do you need new business leads or not? With social media representing 27% of time spent on the web, the potential for you and your business is interminable.

So be savvy and stay away from those normal traps, such as sharing exposed photographs with the internet.

Social media marketing is about imagination — it's the ideal platform for conveying your brand to your intended interest group. Social media has become an undeniably prominent path for brands to convey their one of a kind voice in a casual manner, anyway a few organizations succumb to utilizing the equivalent exaggerated prosaisms in their marketing strategy. These propensities can discolor a brand's notoriety and irritate the damnation out of their group of spectators. When social media marketing is progressed admirably, it can possibly carry more prompts your online business. So what are the most exceedingly awful marketing buzzwords on social media, and how might you dodge them?

1. "WE'RE TAKING X TO THE NEXT LEVEL"

As though your items weren't at that point choice?

This expression is tossed around a ton, and it's in reality all the more harming to your brand and items then you may think. You're straightforwardly telling your group of spectators that your items or administrations weren't that incredible in any case, so you should take them to some puzzling 'next level'.

Related: Why You Need to Optimize Your Site for Mobile Users

Each item you make ought to be the most flawlessly awesome there is, so you're doing yourself an insult by utilizing this one in your marketing strategy.

It's likewise a super-apathetic type of narrating that bears a resemblance to an exhausting Facebook update no one thinks about. If you're making changes to your item or administration, offer some genuine understanding and account into why you made changes, and don't make existing clients feel like they got a terrible arrangement!

What would it be a good idea for you to use?

Be specific with what you are 'taking to the following level', like improving client care or updating your product. If you need to yell about significant changes or upgrades, a network drove post in the tone of "we heard you" sets a superior tone.

2. "IT'S ALL ABOUT VIRAL SOCIAL MEDIA MARKETING"

Everybody is attempting to cause their substance to become famous online, yet let's be honest, just a bunch of businesses will really succeed. To the untrained eye, it appears as though everybody is arriving, however in actuality it takes a great deal of diligent work (and cash) to make your social media battle 'turn into a web sensation'.

The entire idea of making a viral battle is to a great extent dependent on karma. Because you've made a fascinating picture or clever article, there is no real way to guarantee that this substance will spread, except if the planning is correct or it gathers significant levels of commitment on account of key seeding and advancement.

What would it be a good idea for you to use?

Concentrate on making astonishing substance your crowd will cherish, instead of gimmicky crusades. Put resources into an unfaltering marketing strategy that offers steady an incentive for your group of spectators — building trust and brand thought.

3. "Break new ground"

Being absolutely off-brand on social 'for no reason except maybe for fun' isn't constantly a smart thought. From the start, being progressively inventive and giving individuals a chance to have free rein on social may appear the perfect method to reboot a worn out strategy, however you will most likely simply end up with a heap of dissimilar thoughts and messages.

'Fresh' believing is best done during the strategy stage. In business, imaginative reasoning isn't continually something you have to apply to content — it might be that you have to shake up how your social group functions, or the social platforms you're focusing on.

What would it be advisable for you to use?

Thinking excessively far fresh can prompt wacky thoughts – an excess of wackiness could put potential clients off working with you. Don't simply go pursuing wacky unicorn posts — take a gander at how you can run an increasingly spry social group.

4. "THIS IS A 360-DEGREE SOLUTION"

Most likely this isn't what you really intended to state? If your answer or administration that you are offering to clients is 360-degrees, then you will wind up right back in the spot you began from.

There are such a large number of dull and exhausting business banalities out there — don't let your social media channels become the equivalent. It's significant that you center around utilizing genuine language that is immediate and noteworthy. That is path better for clients, and route better for SEO.

What would it be a good idea for you to use?

Change your wording to tell clients why your item or administration truly is different in substantial terms. Giving clients a far reaching perspective on what you bring to the table ought to represent itself with no issue, so don't go after unclear declarations like 'arrangements'.

5. "Quality writing is everything"

In spite of the fact that this one is incompletely valid, the platitude 'quality written substance makes all the difference' has become so dreary that it has nearly lost its message. Without a doubt, content is significant, yet it's not by any means the only part that makes up a fruitful social marketing strategy. Reliably concocting intriguing substance is tedious and it tends to challenge to be inventive. Concentrating on different parts of your social media marketing strategy will enable your items and administrations to catch the eye of your online group of spectators.

CHAPTER 7
TIPS TO GUARANTEE YOUR SUCCESS

It gradually crawled into our lives, gradually. Until it was the point of convergence of our lives.

Today, 7 out of 10 Americans utilize social media, contrasted and just 5% in 2005.

Businesses paid heed, and social media has since reformed the manner in which we do marketing.

The advantages are perpetual with a first rate social media strategy.

A couple of advantages of an incredible social media strategy:

Expanded brand mindfulness

Grow a bigger group of spectators

Interface with your group of spectators better

Expanded site traffic

Create more leads

Profit

There's no uncertainty about it – social media ought to be a fundamental part of your general marketing endeavors.

Simply take a gander at a portion of these enlightening insights:

Facebook has 2.2 billion dynamic clients consistently

Pinterest? 150 million individuals are utilizing this prevalent platform consistently

Instagram is the second greatest social media arrange

It's a huge lake to go angling in for your intended interest group. Not taking part in social media marketing would prompt a deficient marketing strategy.

If you're prepared to kick off your social media strategy, continue perusing.

We're bringing a profound plunge into the best forefront strategies around.

1. Spread out your objectives and targets

Having a strong arrangement, targets, and objectives are basic if you need to kick off your social media strategy.

If you don't have the foggiest idea what you need, how are you expected to accomplish it?

Also, you can't quantify or develop your strategies after some time if you don't have solid objectives in any case.

Your social media objectives ought to line up with your general marketing endeavors.

Recording your objectives is vital if you need to contact them.

As indicated by an investigation, you're 30% bound to be effective if you record your objectives. In certain examinations that number is as high as 40%.

1 Set Your Goals To Be Successful

When you set your objectives, make them achievable and separate them into smaller activity steps.

The most effective method to set feasible objectives to kill your social media marketing strategy:

Use numbers, (for example, arrive at 5000 Instagram devotees)

Continuously set a cutoff time

Be specific and make your objectives "Keen"

Make your objectives in accordance with your whole marketing strategy

Need more help with killing your objectives? Look at Christine's objective setting post here on Blogging Wizard.

2. Research and find out about your group of spectators

Associating and connecting with your crowd is critical in the present marketing if you need to turn a benefit.

In any case, so as to do that, you have to comprehend your crowd – all around.

You ought to have the option to pinpoint their needs, needs, and wants - if you have a desire for making a fruitful social media strategy.

How might you better comprehend your group of spectators?

Study your group of spectators to all the more likely handle their agony focuses

Take a gander at their socioeconomics

Participate in discussions on gatherings loaded up with your intended interest group

React to remarks on your blog, and remark on different web journals with a similar objective group of spectators

Answer to all remarks or inquiries on your social media channels

Gather input (utilizing one of the numerous client criticism apparatuses accessible)

When you discover who your intended interest group is, you're better prepared to support them. They need to manage businesses who care – not only a nondescript brand.

Which makes this a crucial advance in making any social media strategy.

3. Run challenges to amp up your social media strategy

Making an effective social media challenge is one of the most appealing strategies you can utilize. It'll expand your online perceivability, your adherents, and your commitment.

There are various apparatuses you can use to make an extraordinary giveaway or sweepstakes.

The way to executing a fruitful challenge is offering something of huge worth.

Something that will be compelling to your crowd.

Here's a case of a challenge that had incredible outcomes:

2 Social Media Contest Example 1

What's more, another kind of challenge that progressed admirably:

3 Social Media Contest Example 2

Step by step instructions to run a challenge on social media:

Make sense of your objectives (do you need more Facebook page likes? Instagram devotees? What number of?)

Choose what social media channel you'll have the challenge on

Concoct a cutoff time for when it'll end and when the champ will get their prize

Make the challenge (take a gander at different sorts and pick the correct one for your crowd)

Advance it energetically!

To get stunning outcomes, intend to have your crowd do a portion of the truly difficult work.

Set the challenge up so they get additional sections for sharing the challenge or finishing comparable assignments.

For example, "Stick on Pinterest", "Offer on Facebook", or "Like my Facebook page". You can likewise give them a novel connect to share for additional passages.

It's virtuoso. Your challenge will fundamentally run itself!

4. Art your social media content cautiously

Each bit of substance you post on social media ought to be deliberately considered. If you're presenting just on post something – you're turning out badly.

Contingent upon the social system you're posting on, you'll have to gain proficiency with the different reasons for each system.

Here are a few models:

LinkedIn – An expert system that is ideal for B2B crowds. Likewise incorporates LinkedIn Pulse, a substance distributing and circulation platform.

Facebook – Almost everybody has a Facebook account. Especially useful for news/diversion related content. While Facebook Pages battle to perform, Facebook Groups can be an incredible method for interfacing with your optimal crowd.

Instagram – Perfect if your substance is profoundly visual. Static pictures and short recordings work extraordinarily well however it's not as great at driving traffic back to your blog.

Pinterest – Similar to Instagram, Pinterest is profoundly visual. In spite of the fact that it's restricted to static pictures, it very well may be exceptionally effective at driving traffic back to your blog.

Note: For additional on how every social system can fit into your marketing strategy, look at our post on the brain research of social systems.

When you find out about the changing systems, you can concentrate on which ones you think will work well with your business.

A significant part of murdering it at your social media strategy is utilizing the correct words. The manner in which you communicate as the need should arise will shift contingent upon the social system you're posting content on.

Be that as it may, when all is said in done, there are approaches to improve your online perceivability over every one of the platforms!

To specialty dazzling duplicate on social media:

Use copywriting strategies.

Address your group of spectators legitimately.

Utilize smart, clever, or captivating snares to start your social media posts.

Change things up with different substance types (Try connecting to blog entries, recordings, pose inquiries, and so forth).

Continuously compose a portrayal on each connection you post. Never simply put the feature of the post.

If you flawless your social media content, you'll see higher commitment rates, more supporters, and produce more leads and deals.

5. Keep the salesy strategies to a base

Nosy, conventional marketing departed for good quite a while prior, in light of current circumstances.

Individuals would prefer not to be sold as well.

They need to build up genuine associations and associations with you.

That is the mystery sauce to getting your crowd or clients to confide in you.

Also, if they trust you – they'll purchase from you.

Purchasers discover it off putting when brands and businesses post such a large number of advancements.

As should be obvious, 57.5% of individuals thought that it was irritating in this investigation on Sprout Social:

Then again, you can create accommodating content that individuals really need to devour. Content that leads purchasers to your items or administrations – without being pushy or salesy.

6. Exploit video content in your strategy

Except if you've been living under a stone, you realize how intense video substance has become. Particularly in social media marketing.

82% of all buyer traffic will be from video content by 2021.

Along these lines, if you haven't as of now, it's an ideal opportunity to get on board with that fleeting trend at the earliest opportunity!

There are heaps of different approaches to utilize video content in your social media strategy. Be that as it may, live recordings (like Facebook Live Videos) seems, by all accounts, to be extremely popular at this moment.

Here's a depiction of an effective Facebook live by Caitlin Bacher:

6 Facebook Live Caitlin Bacher

Facebook live recordings enable you to associate with your crowd in an authentic manner that is preposterous in other substance designs. Also you can repurpose your live recordings!

Individuals connect by posing inquiries. So you can give them you're not only a brand, by associating with them during and after your live video.

They'll see you're a business proprietor who cares and that will bring a greater number of results than anything. As indicated by Facebook, you'll see 6x the collaboration and commitment with a live video.

Notwithstanding, a blend of live recordings and routinely recorded recordings will be your best be. You'll have individuals rushing toward you.

7. Make staggering pictures

It most likely does not shock anyone that making staggering pictures for social media ought to be a top-need.

You don't should be a visual creator to configuration shocking illustrations for your brand. You can use apparatuses like Canva or Picmonkey to art appealing pictures to wow your crowd.

Your other choice is to redistribute. Numerous business proprietors and bloggers do this – and it's cash very much spent.

Here's a case of a Facebook Group realistic from Wonderlass:

7 Graphic For Facebook Group

Also, another case of a realistic on Facebook advancing a pick in complimentary gift. This time from Elna Cain:

8 Graphic For Facebook Promoting Opt In Freebie

You'll have to make illustrations for:

Spread photographs for every social media platform you have

Pictures for your select in complimentary gifts (you'll need to post these on Facebook at times)

Facebook and Twitter posts

Instagram pictures – (You can utilize sans copyright stock photographs or make a realistic utilizing Canva or PicMonkey.)

Infographics

Pinterest designs

The measurements for these will change after some time. So do your research when making these to locate the correct sizes for social media pictures.

Each business' pictures and illustrations will differ, yet you'll need to make them strong with your brand and consistently attractive.

8. Associate with your group of spectators

If you're not building associations with your group of spectators or potentially clients – it'll effectsly affect your business.

Extending your range is without a doubt cutting edge in your psyche. What's more, the most ideal approach to do this is by interfacing in a real route with your crowd.

This will prompt focused on individuals landing right on your site and obtaining your administrations or items. Social media is perhaps the best apparatus to acquire new clients or customers.

Indeed, 73.3% of individuals buy things or administrations because of social media:

9 People Purchase Items Because Of Social Media

Social media is a useful asset for any marketing strategy. What's more, that primarily comes down to the way that businesses can connect and draw in with their clients such that is inconceivable generally.

Keen approaches to interface with your group of spectators:

Interface in Twitter Chats

Retweet on Twitter

Study your group of spectators

Participate in Facebook bunches with a comparable objective group of spectators

Continuously answer to remarks on your Facebook business page

If you can ace this, you'll begin to see the leads pouring in.

9. Use Pinterest to take your strategy to the following level

Pinterest is the third most prominent social system among grown-ups. What's more, the second biggest search engine other than Google.

Somewhat befuddling, isn't that so? Is it a social media platform, or a search engine?

It's really a visual search engine, that is as often as possible mistaken for a social media arrange.

In any case, Pinterest can expand your site traffic, your salary, and your validity and expert in your specialty.

So if you're not using it to its maximum capacity – you're passing up a great opportunity, no doubt.

To begin with Pinterest in your social media strategy:

Set up a business account

Empower rich pins

Make a striking and catchphrase rich profile

Make significant sheets (use catchphrases as the board's name and in the board portrayal)

Start utilizing a mechanization apparatus, similar to TailWind or Board Booster.

Specialty stick commendable designs

Start connecting on the platform legitimately (just as with mechanization apparatuses - for best outcomes)

This will help become your Pinterest following, and the rest will before long become all-good.

The traffic will start to pour in.

You'll turn into a go-to power figure.

Furthermore, your pay will touch off.

You'll be happy you made Pinterest a need in your social media strategy!

10. Utilize the correct instruments

The devices you pick will decide the quality of your whole social media marketing strategy.

Consider it like structure a home.

If you started by setting up drywall or introducing a deck, it would tumble to the ground.

You have to set out an unfaltering establishment first.

The equivalent goes for your social media strategy. Finding the correct apparatuses will guarantee your strategy runs easily.

You'll have to choose which social media computerization instrument you'll be utilizing to plan your social substance. Weigh up your choices – each business has different needs and prerequisites.

Here's a model a computerization instrument, called Buffer, in the free form:

10 Social Media Automation Tool Buffer

As life-changing as computerization instruments like Buffer may be, there are different apparatuses out there that can assist you with overseeing pretty much every progression of the social media marketing process.

To abstain from feeling like you're suffocating with overpower, investigate social media the board apparatuses to oversee everything for you.

What's more, if you're extremely genuine about your social media marketing strategy, you'll need to screen your quality. There are astounding devices to screen your social media nearness, to help upgrade your strategy.

Regardless of whether you utilize 1 or 5 apparatuses boils down to individual inclination, spending plan, and how genuine you are tied in with making a bleeding edge social media marketing strategy.

Note: At Blogging Wizard, our go-to social media the executives device is Sendible. Get familiar with it in our survey.

11. Start a Facebook gathering

If you've pondered making a Facebook gathering – this is the ideal opportunity.

With the extreme changes happening inside social media – Facebook was hit the hardest. Facebook's calculation changed, making Facebook pages all the more testing to develop or benefit from.

Essentially, Facebook is stating you'll be seeing more from your companions, family, and gatherings in your newsfeeds. What's more, less "open substance, for example, from businesses or brands.

Advantages of running a Facebook gathering:

An expansion in your site traffic

Advance your items and administrations in a non-salesy way

Draw in and interface with your group of spectators in an authentic manner

Fabricate your email list

Develop your business and procure more cash

Propelling and growing a Facebook gathering is a first class strategy to add to any social media marketing plan.

To dispatch your very own Facebook gathering, go to one side base hand corner of your newsfeed, where it says "Make", then snap on "Group".

Next, you'll get a screen this way:

11 Launch Your Own Facebook Group

From that point round out the essential data, and you're ready.

Also, when you're prepared — look at my post on advancing a Facebook. Inside, I share 16 strategies you can use to quicken the development of your new network.

12. Advancement is critical to your whole strategy

You could make the most awesome, quality substance on the web — however if no one gets eyes on it, you're not going to get results.

That is the place advancement comes in.

We've discussed mechanization devices; it's fundamental that you use them for the social media platforms you've decided for your social media strategy.

You'll likewise need to have a different instrument for Pinterest, for example, TailWind.

This'll amplify the quantity of individuals who see your substance and it'll soar your site traffic and your pay.

Making exceptional and various substance for social media is urgent, yet don't disregard the advancement procedure.

This is a huge slip-up that numerous bloggers and business proprietors make.

So what special work would you be able to do to step up your strategy?

Cross advance between your other social profiles

Team up with influencers in your industry

Run a social media challenge that urges members to tail you

Influence different platforms you approach (for instance, after somebody buys in to your email list, welcome them to tail you on social media.)

Adopt a SEO-driven strategy to the substance you distribute on social systems (for instance; utilize important hashtags on Instagram and utilize prevalent catchphrases in titles/depictions on YouTube.)

13. Think about the most recent patterns and changes

Remaining in front of the control is fundamental in social media marketing.

It's eternity changing, and calculations are being adjusted left, right, and focus. Making it your business to remain over the most recent patterns and changes in social media.

This incorporates finding out about current measurements for the social platforms you use, and social media insights when all is said in done.

For instance, here are a few patterns happening at this moment:

Live video substance is just climbing and is proceeding to develop

Instagram stories are a go-to strategy for businesses

Informing applications are on the ascent for a route for buyers to address businesses

Influencer marketing is extremely popular

Computer generated reality in marketing has gotten colossal

Tips for Successful Social Media Marketing that Delivers 10X ROI

A fruitful social media marketing is actually what you requirement for your business to develop.

Social media marketing can be a unique powerhouse that solidifies branding, makes quality leads, and drives deals. Or on the other hand, it tends to be a hotshot squandering, task-arranged flop. The key is to realize how to deliberately make, do, and measure the general arrangement.

Businesses attempting to accomplish fruitful social media marketing must beat a few normal difficulties. Cutting out sufficient opportunity, making high-performing substance, and appropriately estimating the subsequent measurements are for the most part angles that, if took care of erroneously, can tank the arrangement and leave them with a major goose egg as the result.

Try not to do that!

With some arranging, organizations are bound to reach and surpass the result that got them amped up for social media marketing in any case.

Fortunate for you, we have the bit by bit plan spread out.

Pursue these 10 simple tips to shake your social media marketing strategy and appreciate 10X rate of profitability.

1. Identify Your Goals

It's a brilliant business practice to begin with objective setting before every new arrangement, and social media marketing's the same. All things considered, you can be the best bike sales rep in the state, yet at the same time come up short if you should sell frozen yogurt.

Utilize the SMART objective setting strategy to make the establishment for effective social media marketing.

Specific. Dubious objectives like "get more business" doesn't assist organizations with pinpointing their goal and make proportions of achievement. Objectives must nail down precisely what is anticipated from the activity.

Quantifiable. Having the option to conclusively answer "indeed, we hit the objective" or "we missed the objective by 20%" is a decent objective standard.

Feasible. Distant objectives are disheartening and baffling. Extending to hit an objective is beneficial, however don't go over the edge with desires.

Significant. A social media marketing objective needs to attach in to marketing's general objective. Is it to assemble a group of people? Increment site traffic? Strengthen branding? Ensure the objective identifies with the master plan.

Convenient. Dates and times keep organizations responsible to their objectives. Remain on track by separating a huge venture like this into smaller than expected objectives that each have their very own cutoff time.

When organizations set the objective, which is essentially the "why", they have to settle on the "who".

2. Identify Your Audience

Your message won't be effective except if its specifically intended for who you are attempting to target. Building up an applicable purchaser persona is basic for effective social media marketing. Three snippets of data offer understanding into pinpointing your group of spectators.

Survey glad customers. Customers that have been satisfied by an organization's item or administration are prime beginning stages when building a purchaser persona. Concentrate their businesses, socioeconomics, and their objectives near comprehend who you ought to target.

Nail down torment focuses. What question does your item answer? How can it make your purchaser's activity simpler? Just by altogether understanding this can an association show their worth.

Overview client service. Converse with the individuals who are on the forefronts. What are the issues they hear frequently? Knowing this shows you the course to take in the substance that will in all probability connect with and intrigue your objectives.
Presently how about we answer "where".

3. Select the Best Platforms

It's generally a mix-up to attempt to develop adherents on about at least six social media channels. The individual dealing with the social media endeavors gets overpowered, off track, and the outcomes wind up being weak.

Facebook is the social media mammoth, obviously. LinkedIn is likewise incredible for businesses to have a nearness. Be that as it may, neither might be the one organizations should concentrate on.

Who needs the item or administration? The offering is critical to the platforms you ought to pick. Selling straightforwardly to purchasers? Facebook is your most logical option. Focusing on a more youthful group of spectators? Snapchat or Instagram may play out the best. Marketing to different organizations? LinkedIn could be your brilliant ticket.

Where are the contenders? Put your insightful cap on and make sense of which channels your rivals are utilizing. Concentrate their quality, and take a gander at their devotees. It's not necessitated that you be on each channel they are on. In any case, seeing a contender with huge amounts of devotees and commitment should incite you to move that specific social media channel to the highest priority on the rundown.

Fruitful social media marketing sets aside lumps of effort to oversee. It's much better to pick a couple of directs and truly put resources into them than five or six channels and spread the message to far.

4. Utilize a Qualified Manager

It takes one of a kind characteristics to be a canny social media chief. One of the missteps organizations oftentimes make is to pick the individual who has the lightest calendar or the least expensive every hour rate with no respect for whether they are "worked" for the activity.

Key thinking. There's quite often a key scholar behind effective social media marketing. Organizations should take a gander at the contender for the activity intently and talk about the short and long-run objectives. The individual needs to see how to spread out posts, pick content, and draw in with adherents such that works toward progress.

Authoritative aptitudes. Running social media crusades requests somebody that can spread out the strategy in a bit by bit approach. They have to have an idea about their time and control of their schedules. Basically posting "when they consider it" won't do a lot to move the needle.

Branding aptitude. They may not be the "face" of the organization, yet they are certainly the "voice". It's basic for the social media supervisor to comprehend the organization brand at a granular level, have solid sentence structure and spelling aptitudes, and display polished skill in all circumstances.

5. Convey Consistently

An exceptional social media activity is one that is supported continually. Hurling a blog here and an image there won't fabricate a prosperous marketing strategy.

Compose content. Continuously remember the focused on purchaser when sharing substance. Web journals, new white papers, and online course solicitations are savvy decisions.

Clergyman content. Posting applicable industry data and articles composed by others are extra approaches to fill the social media schedule. Maintain a strategic distance from continually posting something deals y. This turns crowds off.

Tune in. Devices that let organizations tune in to what contenders and the intended interest group are keen on and discussing guides them toward what they ought to share.

6. Charm Influencers

Did you realize that practically half of purchasers search influencer surveys when paying special mind to an item to purchase? That is the manner by which huge the influencers' suggestions are. Why? Indeed, most likely because they trust these influencers. These individuals have just settled their validity therefore their proposals matter to generally clients.

So discover who the specialists are about the item or administration you sell. The ones with an enormous after on social media are influencers.

System. Connect with and fabricate associations with these dynamos to arrive at more targets and further grow the branding message.

Broaden an offer. Be set up to answer the "how might this benefit me" question. Perhaps they could go along with you at a public exhibition, or advance themselves on one of your online classes. It's essential to show how you carry an incentive to them as you encourage these connections.

Screen. Watch what the influencer posts about your brand, and make certain it's strong to your picture. If, for instance, they attempted your item and didn't care for it, it's ideal to know this in advance. Continuously speak with influencers and focus on what they state, so there aren't any frightful shocks.

Extra tip: For Instagram, if you need to build your arrive at when teaming up with influencers, use Instagram Stories. This has been casted a ballot as the second most well-known configuration when it comes to influencer Instagram marketing. It really arrives at 500 million clients consistently and is demonstrated to be multiple times quicker contrasted with different sorts of feed.

7. Develop Your Audience

The more eyes that see your message, the more outcomes you appreciate. The social media director needs to take a shot at expanding adherents over all the social media channels regarded pertinent for the item or administration.

Current clients. Satisfy sure current clients pursue your social media. Item refreshes, new substance, and industry data are for the most part important to clients. Do it well, and the message could incite them to purchase once more.

Substance fans. Individuals who stumble into and digest your substance are prepared to tail you. It's imperative to urge them to buy in to your blog, and make it simple for them to tail you for future refreshes. Challenges are incredible approaches to build adherents.

Paid promotions. Natural is marvelous, yet a few organizations additionally select paid promoting to develop their volume of devotees. Promotions are extraordinary approaches to arrive at your purchasers that would some way or another never come into contact with your message. To study paid advertisements, read our 10 Essentials to Running Successful Facebook Ads.

8. Connect with Your Audience

For social media marketing to be fruitful, organizations need to discover approaches to expand commitment in the supporters they have and the ones they need.

React. Social media the board is anything but a single direction road. React actually to new adherents, answer questions and address issues quick, and remark and like different posts.

Tag. If there are adherents you know are keen on a specific snippet of data, label them when you post about it. Demonstrating individual contacts like this helps drive the nature of your social media endeavors.

Connection. Contingent upon your objectives, incorporate connects in your posts. Something else, adherents don't have the foggiest idea what you need them to do straightaway. Connection to online journals, your site, or different invitations to take action (CTA). Urging customers to make a move is key in creating fruitful social media marketing.

Use hashtags. Help the crowd slice through the huge measure of clamor with significant hashtags. Choose ahead of time on a rundown of hashtags that the business will utilize. These are neon indications of the web that help your message be progressively discoverable.

9. Measure Your Results

Close the circle by holding the outcomes up to the objectives you set and perceive how they analyze. Else, you won't have any thought which strategies are satisfying and which ones slammed.

Adherents. Aggregate up the quantity of new adherents every social media platform got, and contrast this number with the objective. Intriguing social media platforms in every case reliably include new adherents.

Preferences/shares/remarks. Measure the measure of commitment the group of spectators has with the posts. It's sure if you are accepting retweets, offers, remarks, and likes. Note which kind of substance gets the greatest reactions.

Snaps. This is the place the measurements begin to show how social media endeavors did, or didn't, start moving the business needle. Were there numerous snaps to your blog entry or site? Did devotees make that next stride? The achievement of social media marketing relies upon the capacity to bring more guests into the business channel.

Downloads. If your group of spectators reacted to your presents by continuing greeting pages and downloading high-esteem substance like eBooks and white papers chalk this up as a triumph!

Leads. Everything comes down to this. At last, effective social media marketing builds the quantity of qualified leads for the organization. This is the metric that informs you the most concerning your endeavors. Show restraint. It requires some investment to sustain outsiders into leads, even with phenomenal substance and steady posting. In any case, they will stream in the end if it's done well.

10. Foam. Flush. Rehash.

Measurements give you where you have been, and they additionally guide out where you have to go. Organizations need to take the measurements they accumulate and use them to rub their message. Does one sort of substance make greater commitment? Is there an example of posts increasing more consideration on specific days, or specific occasions of day? Improves crosswise over one platform over another? Utilize this information to alter and sharpen the strategy. You will see considerably more noteworthy outcomes from social media marketing endeavors.

Fruitful social media marketing represents an assortment of difficulties to businesses, and it's anything but difficult to go astray and end up with not exactly exciting outcomes. It's likewise regular to begin energized, and get wore out and lose duty in your endeavors.

CHAPTER 8
HOW TO CREATE YOUR STRATEGY

The key element for doing social media marketing great is having a strategy.

Without a strategy, you may be posting on social media platforms for posting. Without understanding what your objectives are, who your intended interest group is, and what they need, it'll be difficult to accomplish results on social media.

Regardless of whether you need to develop your brand through social media or to step up as a social media advertiser, building up a social media marketing strategy is basic.

Here's single direction to do it.

Social Media Marketing Strategy: The Complete Guide for Marketers

Step by step instructions to make a social media marketing strategy

It's fascinating to take note of that a social media marketing strategy and a social media marketing plan have a ton of hybrids.

You can consider it along these lines: A strategy is the place you're going. A plan is the manner by which you'll arrive.

Perhaps the least complex approaches to make your social media marketing strategy is to ask yourself the 5Ws:

For what reason would you like to be on social media?

Who is your intended interest group?

What are you going to share?

Where are you going offer?

When are you going offer?

To assist you with making your strategy, I have made a basic social media marketing strategy format. Don't hesitate to utilize, adjust, or modify it as you see fit (in the wake of making a duplicate of it).

Social media marketing strategy format

Here's another fascinating point about strategy (or strategies): You can likewise have a strategy for every one of your social media channels, for example, a Facebook marketing strategy, an Instagram marketing strategy, etc, which all lead up to your general social media marketing strategy.

A pyramid of social media marketing strategies

Be that as it may, how about we start with your general strategy.

1. For what reason does your business need to be on social media?

The absolute first question to answer is the Why.

This identifies with your social media objectives. Is it true that you are on social media to advance your items? To direct people to your site? Or then again to serve your clients?

All in all, there are the nine social media objectives you can have:

Increment brand mindfulness

Direct people to your site

Create new leads

Develop income (by expanding information exchanges or deals)

Lift brand commitment

Fabricate a network around your business

Give social client support

Increment makes reference to in the press

Tune in to discussions about your brand

You'll likely have more than one social media objective, and that is fine.

By and large, it's extraordinary to concentrate on only a bunch of objectives except if you have a group, where different individuals or gatherings inside the group can take on different objectives.

For instance, at Buffer, the marketing group utilizes social media both to build our brand mindfulness and direct people to our substance while our Advocacy group utilizes social media to give opportune client service.

2. Who is your intended interest group?

When you have made sense of your Why, the following interesting point is your intended interest group.

Understanding your intended interest group will help you all the more effectively answer the accompanying inquiries on what, where, and when you are going to share.

For example, if a movement and lifestyle brand (like Away) realizes that its intended interest group wants to find out about new places and travel tips, it could share such substance on its social media profiles.

An incredible exercise to attempt here is to fabricate marketing personas.

There are a wide range of methods for building marketing personas. My undisputed top choice methodology is to, once more, utilize the 5Ws and 1H.

Who are they? (For example employment title, age, sex, pay, area, and so on.)

What are they keen on that you can give? (For example excitement, instructive substance, contextual investigations, data on new items, and so on.)

Where do they for the most part hang out on the web? (For example Facebook, Instagram, and so forth or specialty platforms)

When do they search for the sort of substance you can give? (For example ends of the week, during their day by day drive, and so forth.)

For what reason do they devour the substance? (For example to show signs of improvement at their particular employment, to get sound, to keep awake to date with something, and so forth.)

How would they devour the substance? (For example peruse social media posts, watch recordings, and so forth.)

You likely don't need to begin without any preparation. If your business has been running for some time, you most presumably as of now have a decent feeling of your intended interest group. What may be useful is to record it so you can impart it to the group or use for your future reference.

To assist you with building up your marketing persona, Kevan Lee, our Director of Marketing, have composed a total manual for marketing personas.

3. What are you going to share?

When you see this inquiry, you may be contemplating the sorts of substance to share. For instance, would you like to share recordings or pictures?

Be that as it may, hang on for a second!

We're discussing your social media marketing strategy here so we should make a stride back and think on a more significant level. Rather than the kinds of substance to share, "subject" may be a superior word.

Here are a couple of brands and their theme(s):

MeUndies, a clothing brand, shares photographs from their clients and photographs of their items on their Instagram profile.

Hackberry, an open air and experience brand, shares their article substance and great photographs of the outside on their Facebook profile.

Tunnel, an extravagance lounge chair brand, generally shares images on their Instagram profile.

If you look through the social media profiles referenced above, you may have seen that the brands have more than one primary topic. Having a bunch of topics is splendidly fine as it gives you the space to share a scope of substance to keep your group of spectators connected with without being apparently unfocused.

This is the place a decent comprehension of your intended interest group will be useful. Take a gander at your marketing personas and think about the accompanying inquiries:

What objectives and difficulties do they have?

How might you help tackle them?

For a wellness clothing and extras brand (like Gymshark), an objective of its intended interest group may be to keep awake to-date with the most recent wellness gears. All things considered, it can share its most recent items on its social media profiles.

(Would that be excessively special? Possibly not. Speculation bank Piper Jaffray reviewed in excess of 8,600 American young people and found that 70 percent of them favored brands to get in touch with them about new items through Instagram. The key returns to understanding your intended interest group.)

4. Where are you going offer?

The following stage is to figure out where you are going to share your substance. At the end of the day, which social media platforms does your brand need to be on?

Before we go any further, recollect that your brand doesn't need to be on each social media platforms. We have committed that error previously. Being on less platforms gives you a superior center and more opportunity to make better content.

Once more, your comprehension of your intended interest group will prove to be useful here. Which platforms are your intended interest group most dynamic on? What makes them visit that platform? For instance, adolescents and youthful grown-ups may like looking through Instagram when they are exhausted to perceive what their companions are doing or whether their preferred brands have new items.

Another, but smaller, interesting point is, what is your brand's "X factor"? It is safe to say that you are incredible at photography, recordings, or composing? Certain platforms loan itself well to certain substance types. For instance, photographs are extraordinary on Instagram, long-structure recordings on YouTube, articles on Medium. Be that as it may, this is a minor point because social media platforms are developing to give pretty much every sort of substance these days.

At long last, think about smaller, specialty platforms, as well. For instance, Zwift, a multiplayer web based cycling preparing programming organization, has begun a club on Strava, a social system for competitors. Their club has in excess of 57,000 cyclists, and thousands draw in with their posts on Strava.

5. When are you going offer?

The last key piece of your strategy is making sense of when you need to share your substance. You may be enticed to hop into a research for the best time(s) to post.

Respite. Furthermore, relax.

How about we make a stride back and take a gander at this from a more significant level once more. Before choosing precisely which time and days of the week you need to post, think about the practices of your intended interest group.

When do they as a rule utilize social media to discover the sort of substance that you'll share?

Here are a few guides to consider:

Sports fans are likely on social media only previously, during, and soon after games to discover and cooperate with content about the occasion.

Competitors may be on Instagram while they are chilling off after their morning or night exercises.

Individuals who love to travel may be progressively dynamic on social media during the ends of the week when they are making arrangements for their next outing (or during their work breaks when they are envisioning about their next outing).

Moms of infants may be looking through social media when they are breastfeeding in the night.

You may have surmised from these couple of models that there probably won't be an all-inclusive best time to post. It truly relies upon your group of spectators. So for this progression, center around the general standards of conduct of your intended interest group.

When you have made your social media marketing strategy, you would then be able to discover your brand's best time to post through experimentation.

At long last, how are you going to execute this strategy?

Furthermore, there you have it — your social media marketing strategy!

Yet, that is not the end. As referenced over, a strategy is the place you're going; an arrangement is the way you'll arrive. You have chosen where to go to; presently you need an arrangement.

By what method would it be advisable for you to round out your social media profiles? What should your tone and voice resemble? What posts type (for example picture, connect, video, and so forth.) would it be a good idea for you to utilize?

Social media marketing is difficult.

Nobody in the business should be informed that much.

Be that as it may, "it's hard" isn't a reason for disappointment. This is often the basis advertisers and business proprietors use to disregard social media.

They don't place it in those words however, obviously. Rather, we hear individuals state, "social media doesn't work for our sort of organization," or things like that.

Possibly that is cruel. It's additionally valid. The way to progress begins with pushing past thusly of reasoning.

An excessive number of organizations make social media accounts - and afterward quit when they don't see immediate results.

Others keep up a social nearness because they think they need one - despite the fact that it's not driving outcomes.

In either case, the missing piece is having a social media plan that works.

Furthermore, we can help with that!

In this post, I'll tell you the best way to make a social media plan that will assist you with expanding brand mindfulness, drive traffic, and increment transformations.

What Is A Social Media Plan (And Why Do I Need One)?

This inquiry is not so self-evident. In the least difficult terms, it's a far reaching strategy for your social media marketing. A well-constructed plan ought to include:

An unmistakable rundown of objectives and destinations

A review of your current social media nearness

Focused examination

A fundamental social media content strategy plot

Building a social media schedule

Built up techniques for estimation and investigation

Building an effective strategy for social media requires significant investment. In any case, it's time very much spent!

An effective arrangement is fundamental for guaranteeing the accomplishment of your general social media marketing endeavors.

A social media plan makes a difference:

Keep up reliable posting plans crosswise over channels

Stay away from a minute ago hurrying to discover substance to share

Quit missing the vessel on slanting subjects because of lack of common sense

To put it plainly, an effective arrangement causes you improve and work all the more proficiently... with less pressure.

Set Measurable Social Media Marketing Goals

Before you do anything, you have to realize for what reason you're on social media in any case.

Here are a few instances of shared objectives and destinations:

Drive changes

Manufacture associations with potential clients

Build up industry authority

Raise brand mindfulness

Realizing how to set beneficial objectives is significant!

It's additionally a profound subject deserving of a post without anyone else's input. Luckily, the people at Simply Measured set up together a fantastic post on social media objective setting to kick you off.

Review Your Social Media Channels

Prior to anybody freezes, the sort of review we're talking about doesn't include getting called by the IRS.

We're looking at assessing your present social media nearness and doing some housecleaning.

How about we start by choosing your social channels. This involves:

Assessing which social media channels you're now on

Figuring out which you should keep and which you should surrender

Choosing which (if any) you should include

Inquisitive how to realize which channels are directly for you?

Start by posing these 3 inquiries:

1. Is my crowd on a given channel?

If you're uncertain, there's a simple method to discover - creep on your opposition.

Peruse their social media nearness. Make note of which systems they're on, how enormous their followings are, and whether they seem, by all accounts, to be driving commitment.

2. Do I have the opportunity to put resources into this channel?

Dormant social media channels will leave guests with a negative impression of your brand. Dodge this issue by not taking on a bigger number of channels than you can deal with.

3. Would i be able to tie accomplishment on this channel back to real business destinations?

Social media can bolster various business goals. The key is to just ensure you're purposeful with your endeavors. It's additionally critical to see how those endeavors sway your business.

Upgrade Your Social Channels

When you've chosen the social media channels you'll utilize, the subsequent stage is to streamline them.

At least, this implies ensuring you've completely finished your profiles. These means are not entirely obvious (and they are neglected often):

Are your profile segments completely rounded out?

Have you included connections back to your site?

Are alluring spread photographs set up?

This is basic stuff that merits keeping an eye on before continuing. You may locate some astounding oversights which can be fixed rapidly.

Have A Plan For Creating Visual Content

Talented journalists and social media experts are not really gifted originators or videographers (and the other way around).

In any case, if you're working with a small group (or in any event, working alone) - you might be attempting to make every one of the advantages you requirement for a fruitful social media plan.

Here are some approach to address these normal issues.

1. Not certain how to shoot your recordings?

Shoot video with your telephone! You presumably won't win any Emmys, however most cell phones can shoot video all around ok for essential social media marketing purposes.

2. Try not to have an originator in your group?

Utilize visual computerization devices like Canva and Info.gram. These choices are ideal for non-planners expecting to make engaging pictures and infographics rapidly.

3. Need an all the more dominant picture manager, however can't bear the cost of Photoshop?

Attempt GIMP. It's a free open-source picture manager that recreates quite a bit of what you could with Adobe's product.

Manufacture A Simple Social Media Content Strategy

Advertisers often battle to discover content they can share on social media.

If that seems like you - it might be useful to begin with substance you're now making somewhere else.

Here's a short rundown of things you can share and advance on your social channels:

Blog entries

Points of arrival

Site pages

News declarations

Recordings

Infographics

Photographs

Client Testimonials

Chances are, you're as of now creating a portion of these things. Why not share them on social media as well?

When contemplating sharing substance and connecting on social media, here are a few interesting points.

Don't (Only) Talk About Yourself

Need to lose companions quick? Just talk about yourself. It's irritating.

This sort of self-assimilated conduct is similarly as off-putting for brands.

Nobody needs to pursue a record that lone offers it's own substance. We're discussing social media here, all things considered.

Stay away from this snare by building content curation into your arrangement.

Set up together a rundown of 2 dozen online journals and news sources identified with your industry. Pick outlets that distribute content important to your group of spectators.

Blend curated content into your substance schedule (more on that in a piece).

Adhere to the 5:3:2 guideline for social media

Consider Native Social Video

Video is developing in significance on social media.

This is especially valid on Facebook, which conveys higher perceivability to video transferred legitimately onto the platform (as opposed to share from an outside connection).

In addition, Twitter enables you to shoot video (as long as 30 seconds in length) inside its portable application on iOS and Android.

Set up Your Posting Schedule

Advertisers generally need to realize the best occasions to distribute on social media. In any case, it's hard to discover obvious responses to this inquiry.

Different studies show fairly different information. In addition, different spectators may connect more on different days or times.

We suggest handling this issue with a 2-pronged methodology:

Use information from industry considers as a beginning stage

Utilize your very own information to at last make your very own inferences

Step by step instructions to Find Your Own Best Times To Post On Facebook

Visit your Facebook page. Then, click into Insights and discover the Posts tab in the left-hand route.

You currently have a reasonable image of the occasions your fans connected most with your posts. To increase further experiences, click the Post Types tab.

This will give you how much arrive at commitment you got on recordings, photographs, and connection posts.

The most effective method to Find Your Own Best Times To Post On Twitter

Tweriod is a free apparatus that examines your Twitter adherents to decide when they're most dynamic on the web.

It takes information legitimately from your genuine supporters, giving you an unmistakable image of your optimal occasions to tweet:

The main admonition is it just breaks down up to 1,000 devotees with a free record. Paid plans can investigate up to 50,000+ supporters.

Step by step instructions to Find Your Best Posting Frequency On Twitter
Sign into Twitter and discover the Analytics tab.

Contrast the quantity of tweets with the quantity of impressions you see every day. Observe what seems to perform best. Then, change as needs be pushing ahead.

Construct Your Social Media Calendar

There are basically 2 different ways to construct a social media schedule. One is with a spreadsheet, and the other is with a reason assembled application. Both can be effective for accomplishing the these objectives:

Sparing time by preparing

Keeping up a reliable progression of substance over your social media accounts

Guaranteeing social media messages are suitably coordinated consistently

Making social media creation and the board progressively synergistic

If you've never utilized a substance schedule, how about we accept you'll manufacture one utilizing a spreadsheet.

To make this procedure simpler, we've made a free substance schedule format in Google Sheets. Don't hesitate to make a duplicate.

You may need to add or expel channels to suit your motivations. It may likewise be important to include or evacuate lines depending the quantity of posts you'll make on each channel.

Then, track with these means:

Include your substance in every cell, on every day, for each channel. Make certain to pursue the posting plan you built up in the past advance.

You can either include your genuine duplicate, pictures, and video joins you'll utilize, or just note which times you'll post.

Stir up the different sorts of substance you post.

Abstain from reposting a similar substance too every now and again. Utilizing a schedule makes this simple to keep away from.

Keep in mind the 5:3:2 standard we referenced before when finishing your schedule.

It's as straightforward as that. Also, if you use Google Sheets (or Microsoft Office 365 with Excel), your whole group can see your schedule in one spot.

Venturing up to a schedule application includes a few key favorable circumstances.

Social media mechanization

Worked in venture the board

Simplified altering

There will undoubtedly be a few significant dates for your brand consistently. These could incorporate occasions, yearly occasions or item/include dispatch dates.

There's nothing more regrettable than scrambling to make content for a day or occasion at last (aside from totally overlooking the day by and large).

The arrangement? Pair your schedule with Google Calendar updates. It's anything but difficult to do!

Stage 1: Identify significant dates ahead of time (occasion advancements, any up and coming declarations you're mindful of, and so forth.)

Stage 2: Create a Google Calendar occasion for each date. Set an email update for everyone to caution both of you weeks ahead of time.

Stage 3: Copy the connection to each schedule occasion.

Stage 4: Use a URL shortener to chop the URL down to a reasonable size.

Stage 5: Paste that URL into your schedule.

This tip likewise works for whatever else you're inclined to overlooking.

Instructions to Align Your Messaging Across Social Media Channels

Arranging admirably planned social media battles is close inconceivable without a schedule. Here's the manner by which to utilize one to design your substance crosswise over channels.

Stage 1: Craft your battle content. This incorporates composing the posts and assembling the pictures and recordings for each post.

Stage 2: Paste the benefits from each post into your schedule. It might be most straightforward to incorporate Google Drive connects to photographs and recordings.

Stage 3: Place each post legitimately all through your schedule, applying the ideas we've examined before in this post.

Stage 4: Devise some sort of shading coding plan. You could pick hues to isolate different crusades and curated content. Or on the other hand, you could utilize shading coding to record content posts, video posts, and picture posts.

Here is a case of what your schedule may resemble when it's finished.

By making content early, you can undoubtedly space comparative messages crosswise over channels to evade repetition.

Set up Which Metrics You'll Monitor For Success

A plan is nothing without objectives. Objectives are nothing without information to quantify achievement.

Knowing which measurements to screen is critical to realizing how well you're doing.

Effective estimation is additionally significant for building a case for social media to your chief or organization CEO. If somebody asks how you're driving income, you need to have a smart response.

Else, you may locate your social media plan getting kicked to the check.

This can get profound. So as to be information driven, take a gander at these 5 territories.

1. Supporter development

The greater your clan, the better. Focus on:

Your absolute devotee/fan tallies

How quick you're gaining new devotees/fans

Regardless of whether preferences, shares, and different cooperation's are expanding alongside devotee development

Tactics For Increasing Social Media Followers:
  1. Clergyman.

Offer significant substance and show you're a solid hotspot for quality data.

Lock in. Put yourself out there and participate in dialogs on social media.

Incorporate social media pursue and offer fastens on your blog and site.

Be predictable. Stale social records dismiss would-be adherents.

Start a gathering on LinkedIn (or both). HubSpot has a great guide on the most proficient method to assemble an effective network.

Assemble an extraordinary item or offer an incredible assistance. Social media won't stow away nor make up for having a frail item.

2. Referral traffic

This is likely a major one for generally organizations. Before you can drive transformations, you normally need to drive traffic back to your site.

Step by step instructions to Measure Referral Traffic:

The least demanding approach to follow this is with Google Analytics. Sign into your record, then navigate Acquisition > Social > Network Referrals.

3. Transformations

Driving transformations from social media traffic isn't really simple. Like we've said before, that is no reason for disappointment (not if you need to keep your lights on and a rooftop over your head).

Instructions to Drive Conversions From Social Media:

Run a challenge utilizing a devoted point of arrival to catch passages. Construct a social media battle coordinating your group of spectators toward your change step. Lead pages has an amazing post on the best way to do this well.

Compose social media duplicate that prods an advantage for clicking your connection (without sounding excessively deals y). Your natural social substance shouldn't seem like promoting. Rather than including a hard publicizing style CTA in your posts, have a go at making duplicate that normally allures those snaps. Here's a strong model.

CHAPTER 9
SOCIAL BUSINESS

Social business—the utilization of social advancements as a formal part of business forms—spins around seeing how your clients or partners interface with your business and how you reshape your business to comprehend, acknowledge, and advance dependent on their association. Social business is tied in with incorporating the entirety of your business capacities: client service, marketing, the official group, and the sky is the limit from there. It means doing this to make synergistic advancement and commitment at important, quantifiable levels attached plainly and legitimately to your organization's business targets.

Social Businesses Are Participative

Eventually, social business is about investment with and by your clients and partners in quest for an association that is unequivocally associated with them through cooperation and community oriented procedures. Thus, a social business is often better ready to react to commercial center elements and focused open doors than a customarily composed and oversaw firm. This may happen through cooperation in a social network, a help or dialog discussion, or any of an assortment of other social applications and settings. The endeavors prompting the production of a social business often start with identifying or making an open door for interest with (or between) clients, workers, or partners inside network or comparable social applications.

A significant point to note here is that when social business practices are drawn nearer and actualized effectively, everybody wins. By carrying clients into the business, or legitimately including partners in the plan and activity of the associations with which they are related, an unfaltering progression of at last productive thoughts rises. Perhaps the greatest misinterpretation about social media and the Social Web as respects business critique is that it's everything negative, that the members are on the whole grumblers and complainers. Not really.

In a 2007 Zenith Multimedia study, of the 3 billion or so verbal discussions that happen around the world, consistently, around 2/3 of them include or reference an item, brand, or bit of media. In addition, positive notices significantly exceeded negatives. The truth of the matter is, except if your business strategy is to produce negative remarks—I can think about a couple of outfits for whom that may really be the situation—the Social Web likely exhibits significant open door for building your business and improving it after some time.

Building a social business begins with setting up a network or other social nearness around or in which your brand fits normally—regardless of whether through an easygoing nearness on Twitter, a progressively included Facebook business nearness, or your own locale worked for providers, accomplices, or clients. Component 14, an Indian gadgets parts provider, offers engineers utilizing its index a network that encourages thought sharing, shared evaluations, and cooperation around equipment arrangements. The people group is currently a center part of Element 14's B2B go-to-showcase strategy: The engineer's locale drives new applications, all the more auspicious data shared among engineers, and a more grounded association between Element 14 and its business clients.

Work Around Customer Participation

Despite who the network is planned to serve, solid networks are best worked around the things that issue profoundly to the individuals from the network: interests, lifestyles, causes, and comparable on a very basic level adjusted needs. This applies whether the group of spectators is fundamentally business—B2B people group like Element 14's engineering network or Dell's "Take Your Path" small business proprietors network structure around quite certain mutual needs basic to small business proprietors—or an individual intrigue B2C or charitable or cause related network.

The center components controlling a social business regardless should be something to which the network individuals (clients or potential clients, for instance) will precipitously bond, and that accordingly will urge them to welcome others to join. On account of Dell's "Take Your Own Path," the basic component is the exceptional arrangement of difficulties looked by small businesses. If you've at any point met a small business proprietor, you realize how enthusiastic they are about what they do. Dell has discovered an extremely effective route through the acts of social business to tap this by identifying and serving the necessities of the small business proprietor—for instance, by empowering exchange about fund and interests in business equipment.

Also, smaller networks—ponder the need to arrive at exceptionally characterized gatherings of clients, where individual interests drive solid connections—are prime open doors for social business activities: Again, take for instance Dell and their "Computerized Nomads" program, went for a specific portion of Dell's client base that actually blossoms with the accessibility of an online association. Advanced wanderers are gainful in the workplace or outside of it, keeping in contact with companions and refreshing col-associations on work in progress through social applications as close as the closest WIFI empowered coffeehouse or inn. One of the basic variables identifying "Computerized Nomads" is the mix of lifestyle and advanced instruments, alongside the fortitude to get associated in pretty much any circumstance. Dell equipment controls this and in this manner takes advantage of the roaming lifestyle of these in a hurry experts. It's significant here to perceive that networks like "Computerized Nomads" and "Take Your Own Path" are not characterized by a business or customer or charitable thought process—call this your perspective or need—yet rather by the requirements and wants of the members inside these networks.

Investment Is Driven by Passion

Getting the movement concentrated on an option that is bigger than your brand, item, or administration is basic to the effective advancement of social conduct inside the client or partner base and too inside the firm or association itself. All things considered, if barely characterized business interests become the dominant focal point, if the social association is assembled absolutely around business targets, then what will the clients of that business find helpful? How might this benefit them?

Further, by what method will the representatives of that business come together for the requirements of your clients? At Southwest Airlines, workers are bound together in administration of the client, through an energetic conviction for the opportunity to fl y being a reality for anybody.

To such an extent that when difficulties are out of control or circumstances request it, the representatives wear the personas of "Political dissidents" and actually get down to business in the interest of safeguarding the "right to fl y" for their clients. As Freedom Fighters, they keep the trademark Southwest vitality up: This makes an interpretation of straightforwardly into the positive discussions about this part of Southwest Airlines found on the Social Web. Being a Freedom Fighter is the sort of incredible perfect that joins businesses and clients and the sort of energy—for movement, investigation, or the capacity to go out and vanquish new markets as a business official—that forces Southwest. It's the sort of enthusiasm around which a business voyager's locale can be constructed.

While the first segment utilized network development for instance, the social business rundown point is this: By understanding the interests, lifestyles, and causes that are important to your clients, you can identify the best social pathways through which to assemble associations with your item, brand, or administration. This is the place various generally good natured endeavors turn out badly: Attempting to manufacture a network around a brand or item will often bomb as cooperation is driven fundamentally by publicizing consumption and (costly) advancements instead of by natural intrigue created by and between the members themselves.

In Search of a Higher Calling

The surest method to dodge this snare is to interest enthusiasm, lifestyle, or cause—at the end of the day, to grapple your drives in an option that is bigger than your brand, item, or administration: Appeal to a "higher calling," as they say, one that is deliberately chosen to both pull in the individuals you need to connect with and to give a characteristic home or association with your brand, item, or administration.

CHAPTER 10
TOP SOCIAL MEDIA MARKETING CHALLENGES

With the regularly developing social media platforms, high requesting job and clients looking for consideration on social media, keeping up an equalization on social media marketing has risen as one of the greatest test for a social media advertiser.

Social media directors realize that social media marketing gives a broad reach and carries the advantage of direct collaboration with clients.

In spite of the fact that social media marketing is considered as an effective strategy for coming to and drawing in with clients, it accompanies a lot of difficulties.

With high challenge on social media, it has gotten substantially more difficult for a social media director to get significant come back from social media marketing. There are various difficulties that a social media chief appearances.

Here are Top 7 Social Media Marketing Challenges and manners by which you can beat them:

1. Estimating ROI

Social media marketing isn't saved when it comes to estimating the arrival on speculation. Advertisers need to always assess the systems and strategies that they executed. Actually this has come up as the top most testing perspective for a social media advertiser.

Instructions to conquer the test:

Identify your key execution pointers

Contrast social media objectives with the general business objectives

Contrast and contenders

Set up investigation to follow execution

Doing this is tedious particularly when you need these on day by day and week by week premise.

There's a simpler way. You can pick the correct fit from among many social media the executives devices. With this you will have the option to get the necessary data readily available.

2. Planning a social media strategy

When social media is being utilized by in excess of 3 billion clients around the world, social media advertisers certainly can't disregard social media as one of the top marketing channels.

With that surfaces a tremendous test of planning the correct social media strategy. Brands must put resources into their social media marketing strategies to build commitment and at last get more leads.

Social Media Strategy

Step by step instructions to conquer the test:

Make specific objectives for more effectiveness

Rotate all battles around your group of spectators

Screen rivalry

Track measurements for nonstop improvement

Building your social media strategy is in reality a considerable errand. Social media strategy ought to consistently be developing.

Social media directors should take advantage by building clear strategies that characterize the objectives, measure the goals, identify target group of spectators, research rivalry and screen execution constantly.

3. Getting Followers

Getting more supporters on social media is perhaps the greatest test that each social media advertisers faces. Brands are progressively keen on expanding adherents since they are seen as future clients.

When your adherent tally is less, you are seen as disliked. Low supporter tally likewise implies that your substance isn't arriving at enough number of individuals who might further share it in their circles accordingly diminishing the general reach of your substance.

Adherents

The most effective method to beat the test:

First pursue records to get more adherents

Offer important and educational substance

Draw in with group of spectators

Work together with accomplices to dispatch battles

Getting important and connecting with devotees can be an overwhelming errand for the social media advertisers. Be that as it may, with accessibility of social media the board instruments, for example, Cloohawk, identifying the opportune individuals to pursue is not any more a test for the social media chief.

4. Plunging Organic reach

The quantity of clients on different social media, for example, Twitter, Facebook and YouTube has crossed a few millions. High volume of substance is being made and curated to be distributed on the social media. Be that as it may, the calculations on different platforms are enthusiastic about expanding commitment of clients accordingly making savvy calculation changes to evacuate garbage.

This can posture difficulties to social media advertisers since they often observe a plunge in the natural reach of their substance.

Natural Reach

The most effective method to conquer the test:

Assemble brand authority

Post excellent interesting substance

Post recordings to drive your range

Target presents on ensure that they contact the ideal individuals

The flood of substance on social media platforms has brought about a decrease in natural reach. Subsequently you need to think of innovative methods for giving top notch important substance to your group of spectators.

5. Expanding group of spectators commitment

Social media is utilized exceptionally by brands to cooperate with fans and potential clients. It is an incredible medium to convey and associate with your group of spectators.

In any case, with the expanded utilization of social media, the social media director faces the test of always discover approaches to associate with group of spectators to build commitment. Be that as it may, producing commitment isn't simple. It's only not tied in with preferring and sharing posts.

Crowd commitment

The most effective method to defeat the test:

First know your group of spectators

Offer incredible (content, video and pictures)

Like, offer and retweet posts

Start discussions on social media

Having a social media profile and posting arbitrary substance won't take your brand anyplace. Produce drawing in content that gets the eyeballs of your group of spectators and further pushes them to like it and offer it.

6. Time the board

Social media chief is always battling to fit in numerous errands into a 24-hour day. Dealing with various social systems, connect with group of spectators, make and distribute content, oversee social media battles, and accomplish social media marketing targets can be a serious testing task it when there is so brief period to execute.

Time Management

Step by step instructions to conquer the test:

Plan your day by day schedule

Use innovation to the most out of our workdays

Start utilizing social media the board instruments

Mechanization to decrease time on day by day schedule undertakings

Social media has become an indispensable need for all brands and there is no uncertainty that it is time a devouring movement.

However, fortunately with the headway of social media it has brought forth a great deal of social media the board instruments which offer assistance in conquering the test of time the executives.

7. Breaking down Social media execution

Social media investigation can be a tremendous errand for a social media supervisor. The humongous measure of information accessible on social system makes it near incomprehensible for an advertiser to order valuable information that can be utilized to get familiar with the conduct of your group of spectators. If information the board isn't done properly, then there are high odds of passing up new leads, industry patterns, group of spectators discussions and brand makes reference to.

Social Media Performance

Step by step instructions to defeat the test:

Utilize a brought together and unified platform for overseeing information

Breakdown the information into helpful data

Break down the information for client bits of knowledge

Utilize brilliant social media the board apparatuses

Social media investigation is critical to gauge the achievement of your social media movement. When you direct standard investigation, your brand can pick up by identifying the patterns, finding potential influencers, discovering drawing in substance, and considerably more.

CONCLUSION

Businesses around the globe realize that social media is digging in for the long haul, yet that doesn't mean you've yet gotten the opportunity to place in the time or exertion important to develop an appropriate nearness on the correct systems.

Be that as it may, regardless of whether you haven't advanced your social media nearness, there is still time, and the advantages will be definitely justified even despite the exertion. There are numerous points of interest to developing your brand on social media, including that it can assist you with improving your client support, enable you to speak with clients and prospects on another level, assist you with drawing in your group of spectators and contact new crowds, assist you with building authority, and direct people to your site.

Your social media objectives will decide the measurements that issue to you, and it's imperative to gauge these to guarantee you're destined for success with your strategy. For example, if you needed to build traffic to your site, then you'd need to focus on the measure of referral traffic originating from your social systems.

There are numerous assets you can depend on for measurements, including Google Analytics, Facebook Analytics and page bits of knowledge, Sprout Social, LinkedIn organization pages report, Keyhole, Twitter investigation and watchword reports, Buffer, and BuzzSumo.

The extraordinary element of utilizing Internet marketing is nonstop access. Despite the fact that your retail store may not be open day in and day out, the Internet is constantly open! Customers can peruse your website at any hour of the day, and as an advertiser, you can carefully 'contact' buyers at extremely inconvenient times through email, on the web, and social media marketing.

With the expansion in the openness of web through cell phones, the idea of social media marketing has truly picked up steam, as it is a genuinely cheap and effective method for contacting the intended interest group. The entire thought behind social media marketing spins around making content in different structures, that can be loved furthermore, shared by social media clients inside their systems Some of the social media platforms that are utilized overall incorporate; Facebook, Twitter, YouTube, Instagram, LinkedIn, Google+, Pinterest. About 71% of buyers who have had a decent social media administration involvement in a brand are probably going to prescribe it to other people.

Social media has gotten far beyond simply organizing. From promoting an item, to really selling it on the web, social media is utilized for an assortment of marketing purposes today.

To such an extent, that it has gotten totally important to concentrate on this territory of marketing if you maintain a business or organization of your own. You may realize what you need to achieve and why, yet without a social media marketing strategy, you won't have a specific arrangement on the best way to arrive. For this business needs to build up a strong social systems administration strategies to showcase their brand on social systems administration locales..

We live amidst a 'worldwide interchanges' blast where the utilization of social media between people for individual and expert use is across the board. Social media, to day, is among best open doors accessible to a brand for associating with forthcoming shoppers. What shopper looks for, thinks, loves, like and purchase is critical to the organizations to know and concentrate the purchasing conduct. Each individual has their very own taste and inclinations which are affected by numerous elements. Generally when purchasers settle on buy choice focus on different part of item like quality, cost and brand yet in present time shoppers depended up on social suggestion. Numerous customers are presently utilizing YouTube, sites, Facebook surveys and appraisals to look for suggestion, peer guidance about items and administrations and furthermore about organization. Social media is filling in as a universally handy medium in voyage of the purchaser buy choice. The pattern of on line marketing is expanding step by step everywhere throughout the world just as in India too. So now day's business proprietors are building up a strong social systems administration strategies to advertise their brand on social systems administration locales.